Praise for *Hedgewitch Book of Days*

"Mandy Mitchell's *Hedgewitch Book of Days* is the book I wish I'd had when I was a witchy new mom. Laid out month-by-month, it's simple to pick up and check the lists of magical correspondences when you're in a hurry, but it's also the book you'll want to peruse when you have a bit more time. Each chapter is stuffed full of ideas for spending quality time with your family, ideas for magical works, and simple rituals that can be pulled off in the time you have between chauffeuring back and forth to after-school activities and trying to get dinner on the table. Speaking of dinner, there are some fabulous seasonal food lists and recipes to help you get a jump on them. A fabulous addition to the libraries of both beginner witches and those who've been on the path for ages and want a few new ideas for simplifying. Definitely two (busy) thumbs up!"

—KRIS BRADLEY, author of *Mrs. B's Guide to Household Witchery*

"In Mandy Mitchell's *Hedgewitch Book of Days* the author brings the old Hedge-witch right up to date. Emphasis is on food but also touches on magic—rituals and spells. All is delivered in a pleasant easy-going style that makes the book easy to read and tempting to just dip into on occasion. In many ways the Hedgewitch was the 'true' witch, in my opinion. It's about time we had a good book that focused on that wise one."

—RAYMOND BUCKLAND, author of *Buckland's Book of Gypsy Magic*

"*Hedgewitch Book of Days* is a fantastic find! Perfect for the beginner and a fun, worthwhile read for the experienced, this book explains why we Pagans do what we do along with great ideas of ways to do it. The author's writing style is practical, down-to-earth and full of wry observations that will bring a smile to your face as it enriches your spiritual practice. Recipes, ideas for simple observations of the Sabbats and Moons plus practical insights about Pagan practice and more are highlighted in *Hedgewitch Book of Days*—I recommend this book highly!"

—KAREN HARRISON, author of *The Everyday Psychic*

"Mandy Mitchell manages with ease a rare combination of humor, truth, insight, and usable information about living as witch. Her path is witchcraft as kitchen magic—things that anyone can do while being a parent and running a home. This is a book of real practical magick, written by someone whose dedication shines through every page."

—VIVIANNE CROWLEY, author of *A Witch Alone*

HEDGEWITCH BOOK OF DAYS

HEDGEWITCH
BOOK
OF
DAYS

MANDY MITCHELL

WEISER BOOKS
San Francisco, CA / Newburyport, MA

First published in 2014 by Weiser Books
Red Wheel/Weiser, LLC
With offices at:
665 Third Street, Suite 400
San Francisco, CA 94107
www.redwheelweiser.com

Library of Congress Cataloging-in-Publication Data
    Mitchell, Mandy.
      The Hedgewitch book of days / by Mandy Mitchell.
        pages   cm
      ISBN 978-1-57863-556-6 (alk. paper)
      I. Witchcraft. I. Title.
      BF1566.M653 2014
      133.4'3—dc23   2014023340

Cover design by Jim Warner
Cover image: Blue Fruit Design—Morris, William (1834-1896 British)
Victoria & Albert Museum, London, England
Bridgeman Art Library, London / SuperStock
Interior by Kathryn Sky-Peck
Typeset in Centaur

Printed in the United States of America
EBM
10 9 8 7 6 5 4 3 2 1

*This book is dedicated to the five girls in my life,
my own two babies, Alexandra and Bethany, who make me proud everyday,
and my three "oh so amazing and beautiful" granddaughters,
Fae, Ella, and Ruby—Grandma loves you so much.
You all make the world a more magical place!*

CONTENTS

INTRODUCTION

Picture this evocative image if you can:

You are walking into the forest. The trees tower tall all around you. The path is slippery and muddy and the light is poor. You are with a group of like-minded people and you are all carrying flaming torches as you silently make your way to a clearing in the trees, to a stone circle. The fire is lit; the circle is closed. You all connect within this sacred space. An evening of rituals and magic ensues, with incense, the sharing of beautiful food and thoughts, incantations, and song. Offerings are made and bonds formed.

You spend your days magically gathering herbs in tune with the moon, creating balms and lotions, spells and potions, as soothing birdsong floats through the window of your immaculate witch's kitchen. You are wise and capable, unflappable and ethereal all in one go, with a little mystery and a lot of fairy dust thrown in. You float on a cloud of velvet and chiffon, handcrafting tokens and amulets; you spend many an hour advising friends, with your cat familiar perched calmly upon your graceful lap.

Sounds absolutely wonderful, doesn't it?

Now picture this not-so-evocative image:

The alarm is screaming, as are the kids. Breakfast, teeth, uniform, school run, and so to work. Endless phone calls, traffic jams. Shopping, bills, and bath times. Packed lunches, homework, Internet. Friends, family, and that annoying neighbor with the endlessly yapping dog driving you nuts! The news, the soaps, the endless football season. Washing, ironing, rubbish—oh, and don't forget that litter tray needs changing! Grandchildren's sticky paws and: "Of course, darling, no problem, I will just whip you up an exquisite costume for your play tomorrow! No, I haven't forgotten your trip money or the cupcakes for the school fair on Friday."

You are haggard, sleep-deprived, and endlessly losing things. You have the conversational skills of a two-year-old and the attention span of a gnat. Rather than

Mother/Father Earth, you are just Mum/Dad, bringer of all things needed. Your kitchen hasn't been cleaned properly since the last time the in-laws came and your partner barely receives more than a grunt for the entire day. You're not even completely sure who your friends are, as, quite frankly, you haven't spent time with them for soooo long! You barely make it out of your PJs all day and haven't been able to a read decent book since goodness knows when. As for going out in the evening—well, evenings are for flaking out in front of the TV, aren't they? Is there even a world outside after dark? And then comes the question that puts dread into the heart of every seemingly stable person: What's for dinner?

What do you think? Not quite as beautiful as the first scene, right? But I bet it's more real to you. And that is exactly what this book is about—the reality of living a magical life today, in the realities of our everyday lives. We all long to follow the old ways and traditions of our ancestors, to get back to basics and work our magic throughout our time here. Unfortunately, our families and friends, our work, our pets, and day-to-day life in general all seriously disrupt our plans.

So this is a book for the here and now—a book to help bring a little magic into your home. I want to show you how you can make everything you do more magical, no matter how chaotic your daily life may be from time to time. I want to demonstrate how daily chores can become magical rituals with the potential to enrich and transform your life—everything from the way you form relationships with your family and friends to cooking, cleaning, and healing.

I hope you can dip in and out of this book, taking from it what you will. There are many esoteric books on the subjects of Wicca, Witchcraft, and Paganism. Some of them are wonderful. They go into depth on the magical rituals and ceremonies associated with the path we all follow. But this book is for all of you out there who, like me, want to live in a magical way and want to bring magic into the things that matter most to us—our families, our food, our health, and our relationships. You don't need to be performing ceremonies and rituals all the time, however nice they are. What you need is a pure heart, a good intent, and a basic knowledge of how to use the old ways quickly and effectively every day. There is only one rule in following this path: Harm none. If you follow this, then you won't go wrong.

I think you'll be amazed at the knowledge you already have, just locked away inside, screaming to get out. I hope that this book gives you the confidence to use what you know and to make magic part of everything you do—not just something reserved for high days and holidays, however wonderful they are.

Why Hedgewitchery?

Don't worry, no long drawn-out history lesson here. I am definitely more a student than a teacher. And goodness, my history teacher was sooo boring that he could send the whole class to sleep with one sentence, bless him! But I digress—never a good sign in an introduction! So to get back to our topic, why Hedgewitchery?

"Hedgewitch" is a relatively new term. It refers to the old village folk who were revered in their communities as healers and keepers of wisdom. For women, they may have been midwives; for males, I think they were known as "pellars"—particularly in Cornwall. These "cunning folk" were an important part of the old communities and a certain mystery surrounded them. They were solitary practitioners. Their knowledge of herbal and medicinal laws was unrivaled, and in a time when there was no modern medicine they treated all types of ailments using the things around them. They knew the folklore behind the local plants and put together brews, spells, and medicines from the hedgerow and from their kitchens.

The other important role these "cunning fok" played was as community counselors. They were often trusted to keep secrets and advise on different situations. This is where the term "Hedgewitch" comes from. Not only did these keepers of knowledge use food and plants to help and heal, they crossed the boundary, or "hedge," that contained their community to converse with other realms. Through meditation and visualization they visited the fairies and spirits, and consulted with them or asked questions to help them resolve community problems. This can take some practice! But as communities dispersed and we lost touch with the wisdom of these "wise ones"—these keepers of local knowledge—they came to be reviled as evil witches and were treated appallingly. What threat did they pose? Purely a different point of view, great wisdom, and success!

In more recent times, our families and ancestors held some of this knowledge and used it in everyday life. Our grandparents and great-grandparents probably knew all the plants around them and their uses. They knew the hidden meanings in the food they ate and the things they used. To them, this was wisdom—passed down from generation to generation by word of mouth. Not much of it was written down—after all, there was no need. Families and communities would never disappear, would they?

But today, in our modern era, this is the biggest problem we have. Our communities and families have dispersed like sand in the wind. We don't live together in groups anymore; families don't stay together all in one place from cradle to grave. Communities rarely exist in the way they used to, particularly if you live in a large urban town or city. Today, even living in a pretty rural village can be very isolating. The modern age has reduced communication to words on a screen and all things Internet and mobile. Even the written word is in decline. When was the last time you sent or received a letter?

Technology is a wonderful thing, but it sometimes comes with quite a high price. We are at risk of losing the bond that exists between us, and with it, all that precious old knowledge—knowledge that is no longer being handed down as it once was through teachings and folklore.

This, I think, is where the modern Hedgewitch comes in. We are, in the main, solitary practitioners, but we do still have a community to serve—our friends and families. We have very little time for contact with the outside magical community, but we do now have, thanks to the Internet, a whole world of like-minded people with whom we can converse. So many people are now turning to new "online communities"; they are springing up everywhere.

Most of our work, however, is still done from the comfort of our own homes and hearths, as solitary Hedgewitches of the modern age. Our role has, in a way, become vital in this world—to record and pass on our knowledge to the next generation and to close the gap a little on all the lost years. We can try to return to the old wisdom our grandparents knew and lived by, using simple household ideas that can enrich people's lives. What we can do is to learn as much as possible, and to practice our magical ways and observe all the important times and tides that our ancestors did. We can strive to make life better for others and for ourselves by using the things around us, and also by having an understanding of the reasons behind using them.

Time to make the world a more magical place again, don't you think?

Why Cooking?

We all have to eat. It's a very simple fact of life—and one that most of us think about a lot and take quite seriously. Food is a source of fuel, but we use it in so many other ways as well. Comfort eating, entertaining and socializing, chicken soup for what ails you—the list goes on and on. But we shouldn't just take food at face value. Most foods have a tradition and folklore associated with them, so it makes sense to use them to their full advantage.

No one I know relishes the thought of slaving over a hot stove for hours, cooking up what amounts to an entire day's pay, only for it to be gone in seconds or to be pushed around the plate. Ask any mother or father what weaning their precious baby off milk and onto "proper food" was like. Watch as that rosy glow disappears from their faces as they recall the battles at every mealtime. My granddaughter has this down to a fine art. She scans the plate of food in front of her with precision and brilliant speed. This is usually followed by the word "done," as she picks up the plate and casually drops it over the side of the highchair! It is an inherited skill I think and proves to me the existence of karma, since her mother did exactly the same thing. It is soul-destroying, however—and not only because of all the expense and effort we went to to give the dear little thing a meal.

We, as adults, have a built-in need to feed children; any children will do if our own can't be found. This is why I think I could never leave my mother's house as an adult without being pestered to eat and to take a "goodie bag" of food I neither asked for nor wanted tucked under my arm. I believe this comes with the parental territory—ummm, maybe it's hormones?

Cooking is pretty much as old as humanity. It's the most basic form of alchemy we have—blending things and transforming them into something spectacular. Well, that's the theory anyway! But in this modern time, we all set ourselves up for a fall before we begin. Food is not what it once was. You can never be entirely sure exactly what is in that beautiful ripe tomato in its pretty plastic tray. I do often wonder what happened to all the "ugly" food. You know what I mean—the misshapen carrots and the knobbly potatoes. It seems as if, in this day and age, we are destined to have an identical diet containing who knows what from who knows where, and as for when—well, who knows?

Today, the food seasons have merged and blended into one long-running show with no end. Whatever ingredient your heart desires can be found lurking in a sterile grocery store aisle alongside things that have no earthly reason to be there, given that they have absolutely no chance of growing in your climate! Do we need them all? Well, it is wonderful to have such choice, but surely a strawberry in summer tastes sweeter than one in the winter?

The cook's role, to me, comes down to using a few basic ingredients effectively: seasonal foods, local foods, affordable foods, and free foods. Now, I'm not saying that I don't eat other foods—good grief, no! I am not that virtuous, believe me. Most of the time, I like to use seasonal produce—selfishly, because I know it's at its best and therefore tastes amazing, requiring very little effort from me. I want my local foods to be as local as I can get—whether they come from the garden, from a friend's garden, or from a local shop. Next, I go after regional items, then those from across the nation, and finally, imported fare. But "imported," to me, just means longer in transit, and so less flavorful and more work for me.

Price is a tricky issue too. Times are tough everywhere for all of us, so price will often come at the top of our list of priorities by necessity. Sometimes the money just won't stretch; so, with the best of intentions, we have to make compromises. Let's face it; we are not going to starve ourselves or our loved ones over a bit of food snobbery. Hot, tasty food at the right price is the order of the day, but it does require a bit more effort and a great deal of imagination.

And finally, free foods! These are the very best, and they really should be at the top of everyone's list. Find and forage for what you can; gather it, cook it, and serve it with the knowledge that you are doing something your ancestors did. Why have we forgotten this skill? I know you all think I am mad. "Did you not just write all about the realities of modern life in your introduction?" you say. "Do you not grasp that I don't have a minute to breathe?" you say. "Forage?" you say. "What nonsense!" But I really am that busy too, and I know it does take some effort—but it is free! You can't find usable free food in all months, I know. And fortunately, the season when it's most scarce is the winter, so you don't have to go trudging around in the freezing cold. But if you can get out, preferably with a small child to do the work, do try it!

THE MAGIC OF THE HEDGEROW

I hope all of this sounds very sensible and very doable, for now is the time for the magic to begin! All the ingredients we use in our cooking hold a magical element— an unseen energy that used to be known by all but that has now largely been forgotten. By understanding what that energy is and harnessing it, we can infuse magic into everything we create. For example, when you go to the shop for some shower gel, you stand in front of a vast array of what's on offer—different bottles and labels and colors. How do you choose? Are you a label reader or a sniffer? Either way, you choose the one that suits your needs—fresh lemon, relaxing lavender, blends that tell you they revitalize you or warm you up or cool you down, or even make you super sexy! The herbs and spices in these gels are specifically selected by the manufacturers to do a job, and you buy that product to do that job for you. You already know that if you want a relaxing soak, you buy the lavender or chamomile, not zesty lemon or mint or pepper. We make so many choices about what works to enhance our day-to-day lives; we hold so much of this knowledge already. We just need to put some of it to work and use it magically.

Try, if you can, to return to the days of our ancestors. Cook with fresh ingredients, with love and intent. Use your ingredients to help you in your life. You don't have to be a slave to the stove—nor do you have to be a martyr. Even a simple cup of tea can be made magical if you make it with focus and wisdom. That's why I call myself a Hedgewitch cook!

So welcome to the first book from the kitchen of a Hedgewitch cook. Here, we will ramble through the year together, considering as we go anecdotes, memories, folklore, recipes, spells, and rituals that relate to each month. In each chapter, I'll give you tips for working everyday magic with the foods, materials, and natural treasures abundant in each month. And I'll share some of my own experiences working with these energies as well.

At the beginning of each chapter, I have given a list of foods that are seasonal to each month and a list of correspondences for each month that represent the magical side of the year. I have also included an appendix that gives a list of the magical properties of herbs, plants, and trees for you to use as a reference. These are just my take on things and are in no way intended as exclusive or exhaustive lists. They are given only to show you some possibilities and to make suggestions. As with all things magical, correspondences and properties are different for each person. Those given here are just the ones that I find work for me. They may be useful as a starting point for you, but I have no doubt that everyone will have his or her own ideas. So, my apologies if I've missed something important to you or something obvious. As I said, I do ramble!

Chapter One

—◈—

MARCH

Mad march hares under a bright full moon,
Sunny days are coming soon!
Warming our way into the year
Bringing with them so much cheer.

Foods at Their Best in March

Fruit and Vegetables

brussels sprouts, beetroot, broccoli, carrots, celeriac, chicory, cauliflower, Jerusalem artichokes, kale, leeks, parsnips, purple sprouting broccoli, red chicory, radicchio, spinach, swede, salad onions, sorrel, rhubarb, turnips

Seafood

crab, clams, cockles, eel, hake, John Dory, lobster, lemon sole, salmon, scallops, skate, trout, mussels, oysters, sea bass, winkles

Wild Foods

daisies, dandelion leaves, fat hen, fresh nettle tops, garlic mustard, horseradish, lime leaves, morel mushrooms, sea beet, violets, wild garlic

(Hurrah! The hedgerow is picking up.)

March Correspondences

- *Festival:* Ostara (vernal equinox). Symbols include eggs, seeds, bulbs, spring flowers, and the hare.

- *Full moon name:* Worm Moon. As the snow begins to melt and the ground softens, the earthworms come to the surface, leaving behind their casts. Other names include Crow Moon, Sap Moon, Fish Moon, Chaste Moon, Death Moon, and Moon of Winds.

- *Astrological signs:* Pisces, February 19–March 20; Aries, March 21–April 20.

- *Birthstones:* Aquamarine and bloodstone.

- *Nature spirits:* Air and water beings connected with spring rains and storms.

- *Animals:* Hedgehog, badger, hare, and chickens.

- *Birds:* Song thrush and blackbird.

- *Trees:* Alder and birch.

- *Flowers:* Anemone, crocus, daffodil, violet, and primrose.

- *Herbs:* Broom, yellow dock, wood betony, and Irish moss.

- *Scents:* Honeysuckle, rose, jasmine, and citrus.

- *Colors:* Pale green, yellow, white, and violet.

- *Goddess:* Ostara.

- *Powers:* Energy, growth, new beginnings, and balance.

- *Other:* St. David's Day (Wales), Mother's Day, St. Patrick's Day (Ireland), Easter (first Sunday after the full moon following March equinox).

March is here and all around spring is—well, springing. The hedgerow is picking up and you can't move out in nature without tripping over a new green shoot or a bouncy lamb. The flowers are in bloom and the birds and bees, ladybirds, and those small annoying little gnat things are everywhere. Incidentally, does anyone out there know exactly how the birds and bees "do it"? I have absolutely no idea. It is still a mystery to me; I guess I really did fall asleep in biology all those years ago.

In March, it's so beautiful that you can't help but want to get outside without your coat and feel some warming sun on your skin. Oh, how long it seems since you were last able to do that. This is, of course, assuming that March doesn't roar in like a lion *and* roar out again; it can be a little unpredictable on that front.

In March, nature is still busy at work, but you only get to see it all if you're brave enough to fight your way through driving rain and gale-force winds. That's the way March is, I guess. We all love to see a host of golden daffodils waving gracefully in the breeze along the banks and in our gardens; however, the reality tends to be a host of slightly battered-and-bruised, bent-and-flat, not-so-golden daffodils lying forlornly on the ground. March winds can take your breath away—that's for certain.

Well, we had best get started, my lovelies. And where to start? At the very beginning!

Getting Started

Getting started on your path can seem a daunting prospect, with a wealth of names and labels to contend with. Are you a Wiccan? A Witch? A Pagan? A Kitchen Witch? A Druid? The list is seemingly endless. I hate these labels, because I believe there is no one box that fits us all; we are all individuals and, whatever your faith and beliefs, they are as individual and personal to you as your personality or your fingerprints. I call myself a Hedgewitch, because I feel this is the image that best describes me. However, I reserve artistic license to believe in what I like—as you should.

That being said, where on earth do you begin to learn your craft, whatever you have chosen it to be? In the old days, crafts were learned by word of mouth and practical methods that were handed down from generation to generation. These days, this has become almost a thing of the past. But the modern age has a trick up its sleeve to replace it—the Internet. Like it or loath it, the Internet is going to be with us for a very long time, and it can be a wonderful aid to getting you started. Out there, in the unseen world of Computerland, are people like you and me, searching for friends and kindred spirits with whom they can converse and share knowledge. With a few simple clicks of a mouse, you can connect with like-minded people all over the earth. You can share your views and beliefs, join clubs and covens, and "like" and follow pages that speak to you. It's like having a Book of Shadows at your fingertips and on speed dial.

If you have access to a computer and the Internet, use them! We are blessed to have this wonderful way of communicating with each other. We witches are an adaptable bunch and should embrace the modern and the new with as big a hug as we do the traditional and ancient. It seems to me that we should move with the times. Who knows? In another thousand years, our relatives may look back in wonder at the "old way" of doing things online!

With so much on the Internet to explore, you may ask what place books have in this mix. (No, no, no; that is not a cue to stop reading this one. Come back!) Books are where I started to learn about what I do, and my bedside is never without a half-read book. The feel and smell of a new book is something so special to me; it touches all those old feelings from childhood. I loved to read and remember receiving a wonderful big book on wild plants for my eighth birthday that I still have today. I have no idea why I was given such a book, as I can't ever remember showing any particular interest in wild plants as a child. But over the years, that one book has been a massive source of reference for me. So there must, I think, have been a higher reason why it was given to me.

For all the resources on the Internet, books are still the first thing I reach for when I want to absorb knowledge. The joy of reading something that has come from one person to another comes second only to the pleasure you get from owning a book. Books are real and tangible—always there to pick up and dip into and reread as many times as you like. The written word, although certainly not as popular as it once was, is still used by everyone, everywhere. Harry Potter, for example, has given me many a quiet evening while my girls buried their heads in the magical wizard-filled realm of Hogwarts.

So as you start on your path, read anything and everything you can get your hands on and then read it again. When you gravitate toward books of a similar category, you start to find that the terms used in those books become familiar to you. Take what you can from these books and absorb what's important to you. This will increase your general knowledge of your subject and give you the point of view of others, which is always a good thing. You don't necessarily have to agree with what an author says. Remember, we are all different. As you read more and more, you will find that you are building a small reference library of your own; one book seems to lead to another. After a year of reading, you may find that you have started choosing books that go into more depth on the subjects that have spoken to you. For me, that old book of wild plants and a good book on herbs were a great starting place for learning what was around me.

The best way to get started, however, is actually to start! Show an interest in what's around you where you live, and if you can, visit some ancient sites and woodlands. I happen to live in one of the most beautiful parts of England—in the county of Wiltshire just near the ancient stone circle known as Avebury Henge. This is actually the largest stone circle in Europe and draws many tourists and visitors each year. It's a peaceful place, where I've watched the seasons change throughout the years. The old stones stand in the fields watching the passage of time; they remind me of the magic that exists in everything that surrounds us.

Avebury Henge is just one of the sacred places I visit from time to time. I suppose that, having it all on my doorstep, I may sometimes take it all for granted—particularly when real life gets in the way. There's also a sacred spring called Swallowhead Spring not far away and a huge earth mound called Silbury Hill that rises up from the ground, creating a dramatic focus in the landscape.

One of the things I enjoy most is going to our community shop, run by volunteers from the village. It stocks local products from around the county. It's so nice to buy bread, cheese, meats, honey, and milk that help support local people and cottage industries. I feel very blessed to live in such a magical and beautiful place.

Another way to get started is to light a candle or some incense and give thanks. Cook and run your household with love and intent, and the rest will come to you in its own way in its own time. Never doubt how much you already know. If you're interested in herbs, start simply with one or two dried culinary herbs that you know are safe, and learn all about them. The same goes for crystals and colors, and for spells and rituals. Record all you learn and see in your own Book of Shadows. My Book of Shadows is a collection of recipes and spells that can be used for everyday needs. I try to keep it as simple as possible. Take your spiritual journey slowly and trust yourself. Even when working on your own, you are a part of the bigger picture—and an important one at that! The power is within you, not without. Remember, harm none. And, if in doubt, shout! Someone will always hear you.

So, provided the weather is being kind, let's begin by getting off the sofa.

March is the time of year when you start to venture out into the big wide world again. After years of practice, I know never to leave my house without a bag or a basket to carry the fruits of my foraging. You can be sure that, if I forget that bag or basket, there will be a treasure trove of goodies for me to gather and no way to carry them home. Try leaving a small basket by your front door to remind you to take it out with you.

The following recipe is a great one to start your foraging. But be sure to bring gloves and something to carry your finds so you are not stung by the nettles.

 ## Spring's Sprung Salad (serves 2)

This is a throw-together recipe that I love to use at this time of year. It has no rules, only guidelines. Use what you can find and judge your amounts by eye. It is a perfect celebration of all things green and leafy. Remember, it is a salad, so your greens only need moments in the pan. For greens, you can use nettle tops, cleavers, wild garlic, garlic mustard, dandelion leaves, daisy leaves, or fresh spinach. For seeds and nuts, sunflower seeds, poppy seeds, pine nuts, cashew nuts, and walnuts all work well. And always make sure of what you're picking—if in doubt, leave it out!

Ingredients

4 large handsful of leafy greens

A large handful of seeds/nuts

2 tbsp. vegetable or olive oil

1 tbsp. honey

1 tbsp. cider vinegar or lemon juice

Salt and pepper

Method

1. In a frying pan over a medium heat, combine the oil, honey, and lemon juice or vinegar. Heat together until hot and add a good pinch of salt and pepper to taste.

2. Add the nuts and/or seeds to the hot dressing in the pan and lower the heat to warm them through without burning.

3. Toss the green leaves into the pan and remove from the heat. Turn the leaves over to coat with the dressing and combine with the nuts and seeds. Make sure any nettle tops have been exposed to the heat so they lose their sting.

4. Serve immediately to retain the crunch of the leaves.

This makes a wonderful lunch or starter. I like to serve it with warm pita bread. Throw in whatever you have on hand in the fridge, too. Celery, spring onions, and lettuce all work well with the bitter greens. It is beautiful with shaved Parmesan cheese. Oh, and for a warm cozy glow of delight at how clever you are at foraging—a glass of red, anyone?

A Time of Balance

March is the month that we've all been waiting for. After the long cold winter, the spring equinox is upon us and the light reaches that wonderful balance point again. Only, this time, the light wins and our days, slowly but surely, start to get a little bit longer each day. The festival of the vernal equinox (*ver* in Latin means "spring"; *equinox* means "equal night"), or Ostara, marks the time when we celebrate the return of the sun. It happens around March 21 and signifies the first official day of spring—although we've been celebrating it since Imbolc, haven't we? In the U.K., March is also the month when our clocks jump forward an hour—the start of British Summer Time. (Now, hang on a minute. Isn't it spring?) So prepare to lose an hour's sleep and have children and animals on a different time than you are. Their bodies never follow the hands of the clock!

The symbols of this time of balance are the March hare, the egg, and fertility in nature. In the family home, this is the time when the dreaded holiday Easter arrives and the house appears to be taken over by an invading army of chocolate bunnies and eggs by the hundred weight! The little darlings are home for their school holidays again, and every year, it seems as if those holidays get longer. I'm sure I don't remember having all that time off in my school days, do you? But it can be wonderful to have the children home for a few days at this time of year, especially if you are blessed with good weather. There are normally lots of things to do and many day trips you can take—laid on mainly for the sanity of mums and dads. Easter egg hunts, lambing at the local farm, and craft fairs all beckon you and push you hurtling toward spring—whether you're ready or not!

I remember one particularly bad Easter when daughter number two announced that she needed an Easter bonnet for the last day of term—which, of course, was the following day. I naively threw myself into this task, stitching fluffy chicks and bows onto an old straw bonnet between rounds at the convalescent home where I worked. The next morning, I proudly presented my daughter with the finished bonnet, bedecked in everything that had anything to do with Easter. Off she went to school.

Foregoing any sleep after the night of crafting and work, I duly arrived at school for the end-of-term Easter assembly, secure in the knowledge that my supreme effort would ensure that my daughter would win the prize for the finest bonnet ever in the history of mankind. Wow, was I wrong! As all those sweet little children filed into the hall, I found myself staring open-mouthed at the creations that bobbed along on their little heads. Honestly, if I had made my child wear a real bunny on her head holding an Easter egg in its paws, she still wouldn't have won! The winner was an amazing creation of a well-known chocolate egg, complete with real chocolate for the children to break off and eat. I learned two valuable lessons that year: First, parents can be amazingly competitive, and second, I am rubbish at crafts! Bake sales and cake stalls? No problem. Bonnets and costumes? No way!

The symbol of the egg is a link to Ostara and the origins of Easter. Eggs are life and fertility all tied up in one neat little bundle. Imagine all of nature's life-force curled up tight in that eggshell, ready to crack the surface—shaking off the old and emerging as new life awakening. It's the perfect symbol for this time of year, don't you think? Eggs, however, always make me think of that old saying about teaching your granny to suck eggs. I have no idea how to suck eggs, and blowing them to ready them for decorating is a rare skill that I don't possess. Because of this, any decorated egg in my house is either chocolate (always better), or colored.

Simple Ostara Altar

It is wonderful to create a focal point for spring festivals if you can, especially if the weather is keeping you inside more than out. Here are some ideas:

- *Decorate with flowers.* Remember, in the U.K., it is against the law to gather wildflowers. So go for a bunch of daffodils or tulips—unless you have a garden full of primroses and violets, that is.

- *Light pastel-colored candles.* Green, blue, pink, or yellow are good, but white works beautifully too. Use flower-scented incense like jasmine, honeysuckle, or rose. Keep it light and fresh.

- *Color eggs for focus.* They symbolize fertility perfectly. I find it's always best to hardboil them before coloring them, mainly due to the random swishing of my cats' tails as they go off on their mission to dismantle my beautiful altar and play catch with the eggs across the floor. Believe me, I have only been caught out once using an uncooked egg. Very messy; never again! You can color your eggs however you like, but remember that eggs are porous and will absorb anything you put them in. So be sure to use natural dyes and inks if you want to eat them afterward. Try boiling them with onion skins, beetroot, or red cabbage, or set them in fruit juice. This can be a great project to experiment with, especially with children. If all else fails, use chocolate eggs, if you can be trusted to leave them alone!

- *Include a dish of water.* Add one of salt or earth as well, to bring all the elements into balance. Spend time making your altar look just the way you want it. Try to remember balance when placing your items, rather than shoving them randomly around each other. Then, when you're ready, light your candles and incense and take a few deep breaths. Focus on the balance you may need to bring to your life, just as Ostara brings balance once again to the natural world.

- *Write down ideas or plans.* You probably thought of a lot of them over the winter months. And write down anything you want to change in the coming season.

It's all about renewal and rebirth, so this is a wonderful time to reaffirm the path you are on. Use simple phrases like: "As the Wheel of the Year turns, I reaffirm my place as part of its cycle." Then burn your piece of paper safely in the candle flame or bury it for the earth to recycle.

- *Plant seeds.* Because Ostara is all about renewal and rebirth, it's a wonderful time to start planting and sowing. So consider planting a seed or two—either in your garden or on your altar itself. Empty eggshell halves are wonderful little containers for cress seeds or for starting off some herbs.

It is always a great idea to do something after your focus at the altar. Use that feeling for something positive. I know—let's go and cook.

Baked Eggy Custard

This is a dish my mum used to love. She made it all the time, but I was never really that keen on it until I added the lemon curd layer. This transforms a simple baked-egg custard into a wonderfully fresh but warming pudding. Perfect for this time of year.

Ingredients

3 eggs, plus 1 extra egg yolk

1 tsp. vanilla extract or the inside of a vanilla pod

450 ml./15 oz. cream

60 g./2 oz. caster sugar

Approx. 4 tbsp. lemon curd

Freshly grated nutmeg for the top

Fresh primrose flowers and violets to decorate, if you have them

Method

1. Preheat the oven to 170°C /350°F.

2. Spread a generous layer of lemon curd over the bottom of a 1-liter/ 1-quart baking dish or place approx. 1 tbsp. in each of 4 ramekins.

3. Beat the eggs, egg yolk, and vanilla extract together lightly, so they are well-combined but not frothy.

4. Place the cream in a pan with the sugar and stir to mix. Heat to just a simmer, then pour onto the eggs and stir to combine. Strain gently through a sieve into the baking dish or ramekins, on top of the lemon-curd layer.

5. Stand the baking dish or ramekins in a roasting pan half filled with hot water. Sprinkle the top generously with freshly grated nutmeg.

6. Bake for approx. 30 minutes (around 15–20 minutes for ramekins). The custard should be set, but it should still wobble a bit.

7. Serve warm.

Ginger biscuits work well with this pudding if you fancy an extra crunch. And remember, it's just as good served cold.

POWER ANIMALS AND FAMILIARS

Power animals, although shamanic in origin, are something that many people believe in. As humans we are somehow programmed to react to animals in certain ways. Who can resist a cute kitten or snuffling puppy? We bring animals into our hearts and homes and so it kind of makes sense to bring an animal in as your spiritual companion too. Whatever power animal you have, it is there with you to lend you its valuable attributes as and when you need them, and your power animals can change depending on your circumstances and what you need at a particular time.

Finding Your Power Animal

So how do you come across your power animal? Here's a really simple way to connect with your power animal.

First, find a few minutes of peace, if you can, and light a simple candle. Take a couple of deep breaths and close your eyes. Say to yourself:

I come to this space to meet with my animal companion.
May it come without fear and bring with it anything that will aid me in my life.

Sit quietly and see what your mind's eye brings to you. It may be an animal that seems to have no connection to you, or it may be something very familiar. Just go with what's there. In your mind's eye, ask the animal to show you anything that it feels may aid you at this time and follow the direction in which it takes you.

Once you have spent some time with the animal, thank it for its presence and time with you and ask it to stay with you in your everyday life. Open your eyes and take a few deep breaths. Allow your candle to burn away safely if you can, or extinguish it with thanks for what you have been shown. This simple practice can be done as often as you feel you need it.

You may find an animal that takes its place next to you for life, or you may be shown an animal whose virtues you need at the moment. How do you tell? Well, one way is to think about the animal you have been shown. Is it a real earth-based animal or an animal that does not walk this earth? Is it a bird? A fish? A dragon? Really think about what the animal means and represents to you. As a rough guide, all winged animals relate to air and your thoughts; aquatic animals relate to water and your emotions; reptiles relate to fire and your passions; earth-based animals relate to circumstances. Any mythical creature relates to your inner spirit.

The animal you have met in your mind's eye will have been shown to you for a reason, so think about its strengths and, if you're not sure, do some research. Is it power you have been shown? Beauty? Wisdom? Cunning? If you have been given a life-companion animal, find out as much as you can about it. It is there to aid you through life and may represent the part of you that needs the most help.

Finding Your Familiar

Many of us have an animal familiar as well as a power animal. A familiar is an animal that lives with you and lends its presence to all you do. I have four cats—all black (except for Merlin, with his white patches)—and each one is as mad as the others. But only one of them is my familiar. This is not to say that you can't have more than one familiar—the more the merrier, I think. But the role of my familiar is taken by my very beautiful black cat, Peggles. She is such a strange girl. She is very timid and I'm sure has an anxiety disorder, as she is prone to hair removal via over-grooming! Peggles is five years old now and she has held her position as my familiar since the loss of my beloved dog, Bonnie, who fulfilled the role for twelve years.

So how do you recognize your familiar? Well, in the case of Peggles, it is her complete change of character whenever anything magical is afoot. The normally timid Peggles all of a sudden comes to the forefront of things, meowing and purring at top volume, paddy-pawing and rubbing against any magical working or tool. She comforts me when I am not well—sometimes with a little too much enthusiasm—and goes nuts at the time of the full moon. Believe me, if you have an animal familiar, you will know it! It may be a pet or a garden animal that comes out to greet you every time you gather herbs or do the weeding. Whatever and whoever your familiar is, cherish it. It will bring its energy and guidance to all you do.

I do think that the local frog population is trying to get in on Peggles's act a bit, too. They always make me jump when they appear in front of me in the garden. Or maybe they're just trying to warn me off their patch.

Spring Cleaning

The increase of light and all the new fresh growth out in nature can only mean one thing for us mere mortals—spring cleaning time! It is at this time that the sun starts to peek through the windows and illuminates all the lovely cobwebs, dust, and smears throughout the house. Windows that have been shut up for the winter are suddenly opened to allow a change of air, and suddenly, you feel a compulsion to clean. Well, that's the theory anyway! Out with the old and in with the new and all that.

I have to admit that I am a bit obsessive-compulsive when it comes to cleaning. My family despair when asked to help with chores, as they know I will probably be behind them within five minutes redoing what they've done. I just can't help it; I seem to be struck by itchy fingers when it comes to dust and dirt. My own favorites are light switches and skirting boards. I'm sure you must have yours—or is it just me who's completely weird?

These days, there are a wealth of products on the market that claim to tackle grime and dirt, and promise you gleaming results every time. There's a different product for each room and then a different product for each surface in each room. The list goes on and on. And while I'm sure that they all have their own merits, do we really need to be using so many harmful products? Not to mention the cost! As a bit of a clean-freak, I want things that will do the job. As a Hedgewitch, I want something natural and safe for the environment. As a wife and mum and grandma, I want something affordable. So my cleaning products consist of white vinegar, salt, lemons, oranges, herbs, baking soda, and vegetable oil. Now, I know these sound like the ingredients for some dodgy cake, but bear with me here.

White vinegar is cheap and can be used as the base for a general cleaning spray. Just fill a jar with some orange or lemon peel and top off with the vinegar. Leave the mixture to infuse for a couple of weeks and decant it into a spray bottle to use as an all-purpose surface cleaner. Or add to hot water for washing the windows. The vinegar cuts through any grease or lime scale, so hard-to-clean areas like faucets or around the dreaded toilet bowl can be treated with neat vinegar.

Here are some more ideas:

- *Vegetable oil.* Infuse vegetable oil with lavender, rosemary, or thyme for a couple of weeks and use this to polish any natural-wood furniture or surfaces. This feeds the wood and brings it to a beautiful shine without applying an artificial layer; it also allows the wood to breathe. The herbs you use will add a lovely fragrance; add essential oils instead of fresh herbs for an instant result.

- *Salt.* Use salt as an abrasive, and add lemon juice to make a powerful antibacterial scrub for your chopping boards, bath, or stubborn sticky marks. Make sure you rinse well after using it, however, or else your food will taste like dodgy tequila! A paste of lemon juice and salt is also wonderful for cleaning copper and brass.

- *Baking soda.* Try sprinkling your carpets with baking soda and fresh herbs. Leave it for 15 minutes, then vacuum. This makes a great deodorizer.

- *Bring in the outside.* Fill a vase with fresh flowers and open the windows. This will work better than any commercial air freshener on the market.

- *Balloons.* My top tip for those hard-to-reach cobwebs! Drape a damp cloth over a balloon and throw it up against the cobwebs. They will attach to the cloth and the balloon will float back down to you. The kids love this one!

- *Deosil motion.* Try, if you can, to clean your home in a clockwise (deosil) motion. Use this same motion when polishing and scrubbing as well. This empowers what you are doing with positivity.

Now all this being said, I am a typical woman and not immune to the virtues of a new cleaning product. Rarely, however, do they deliver what they say, so I do always seem to revert back to the natural stuff that works. But let's be honest. There are some things only a commercial cleaner can tackle—the aftermath of car sickness comes to mind! I don't beat myself up about using modern products around my home and neither should you. I'm sure our ancestors would have jumped at a cleaning product if one had been available. Think how many hours of scrubbing they could have avoided if they'd just had some detergent powder!

CLEARING NEGATIVE ENERGY

Once you've physically cleaned your home, make time to clear its energy as well. All those arguments and conflicts, silences and moods, injuries and illnesses that have built up in the air over the winter need shifting. And scrubbing floors will only do so much. Now's the time to bring out the Hedgewitch in you and really clear the air, so to speak. When you clear your home of unwanted energies, you start with a clean slate. And herbs and incenses are the best way to tackle this.

The classic time-honored way of cleansing the air—whether for magical purposes or for simple energy clearing—is a smudge stick. This is a bundle of white sage tied together and set alight, then stubbed out so the end smolders. The smoke that is produced is wafted around a person or a space. Personally, I have to be honest and say that I hate the stuff. To me, it smells vile—a cross between old ladies' handbags and cheap tobacco. If it's your thing, then use it. Otherwise, there are many other things that can do the same job and smell a whole lot nicer.

Incense is a wonderful way to clear the energy in your home. It is available both in loose form and as sticks or cones—the latter are easier to use. Stick incense and cone incense are made from a mixture of a carrier and oil compressed onto a stick or into a cone. They are easy to use and portable, and they smell wonderfully like the thing they say they are. This has the advantage of making a particular scent readily accessible. And they don't require charcoal to burn, making them safer to have around—although nothing burning or smoldering should be left unattended. But then, you already knew that!

You can make two types of incense—simple or a combination of scents. A simple incense is just what it sounds like—one plant normally burned on a charcoal block—although you can, with care, use the stove top as well. By mixing two or more plants or resins, you can create combination incense and use the properties of each plant to do a specific job for you. The alchemy of mixing your own incense can be fun and magical, creating something very personal to you. The energies of the plants in their purest form can be used in combination to clear you and your home. And each combination will be totally unique.

If you fancy having a go at mixing your own incense, start simply—maybe with something like rosemary and sage, or nettle and lemon zest. See what works best for you. Remember, however, that if you choose to make your own incense, especially for clearing, it will rarely smell anything like the actual plants you are using.

A Simple Home Energy Clearing

Open your windows and doors if you can. (Watch out for escaping pets. Alfie the Hedgewitch dog never misses an opportunity to run!) Starting at the front door, light your chosen incense and say:

May this home be cleared and blessed.

Now work your way through the house clockwise. In each room, hold the incense aloft and repeat:

May this home be cleared and blessed.

If you have time, focus on the smoke touching each corner of the room. After visiting each room, return to where you started at the front door. Allow the smoke to waft over the door and say:

This home has been cleared and blessed, so mote it be!

Now, I know this is a really simple energy-clearing practice and, of course, it can be made as elaborate as you like. But for me, this works and doesn't require wandering round with a piece of paper trying to read or remember a long spell. I think that if you keep things simple, you're more likely to make them part of your life.

Don't get me wrong. I do love all the flourish and ceremony of ritual, but I simply don't have time to do it every day. Besides, over the years, my memory has dwindled to the size of a walnut and I do believe that reading something can take away the focus of actually doing something. Know what I mean?

Once you have cleared your home with incense, there are a couple of other things you can put in place to keep those energies clear:

- *Salt.* Place a dish of salt on the kitchen table. It helps absorb any high emotions that spill from those long conversations over a cuppa. Add nine dried bay leaves to the dish to give its power an extra boost.

- *Onions.* Cut an onion in half and place the pieces around the house to absorb the energies. This is also a wonderful way to keep the air free from bugs and viruses, although it's not one I use often, as it's definitely not the world's greatest air freshener!

- *A bell.* Keep a small bell handy to ring whenever you feel the need to clear the air. Sounds daft, but try it. The noise seems to chase the negativity away.

- *Plants.* Add houseplants to your home. Their living, breathing presence can make all the difference in a room. Just make sure they are securely placed. Many a curse has left my lips and filled the air with negativity as I watched a precious specimen hit the just-cleaned shiny floor—all thanks to a muddy-pawed feline friend, usually Merlin!

Lemons, Salt, and Magical Powder

All the spring cleaning this month brings my mind to three things: lemons, salt, and baking soda. I use them all daily—not only in my cleaning, but as three of the most important ingredients in my kitchen or on my altar. There is so much you can do with these three lovelies, but here are a few ideas.

Lemons to Purify

Lemons didn't become widely known until the Middle Ages. They are wonderful purifiers and can bring life to recipes or spells. Here are some ways they can be used around the home:

- *Litter box.* Get rid of litter-box odor by leaving cut lemons around the box to neutralize any smells. This is a favorite of mine.

- *Floors.* Wash your floors with lemon juice and hot water to deter any creepy crawlies and make everywhere smell gorgeous.

- *Moths.* Hang a sachet of dried lemon rind in the wardrobe to get rid of moths.

- *Hardware.* Polish your faucets with lemon rind, then rinse and dry them with a paper towel. They will gleam.

- *Tarnish.* Clean tarnished brass, bronze, copper, and stainless steel with a paste of lemon juice and baking soda. Allow the pieces to soak, then wash well.

- *All-purpose spray.* Mix lemon juice, vinegar, and water in a spray bottle and squirt away.

- *Fingernails.* Whiten your fingernails with lemon juice. Soak for a couple of minutes, then rinse clean.

- *Fruits and vegetables.* Squeeze lemon juice over cut fruit and vegetables to stop them from turning brown.

- *Deodorant.* Use lemon juice as an emergency deodorant. I haven't actually tried this one. I think it might get a little sticky!

- *Chopping boards.* Rub a cut lemon over your chopping board to clean it after use. It will cut through any grease.

- *The fridge.* Fill half of a squeezed lemon with salt and place it in the fridge as a deodorizer.

- *Blemishes.* Dab lemon juice onto blemishes to help dry them up.

- *Sore throats.* Mix a tablespoon of lemon juice and a tablespoon of honey into hot water and drink to help relieve a sore throat.

- *Rice.* Keep simmering rice from sticking to the pot by adding a few drops of lemon juice. This can make clean-up a lot easier.

- *Rashes.* Use lemon juice neat on the skin to relieve really itchy rashes.

- *Soups.* Add a squeeze of lemon juice to any soup to lift and compliment the flavor. This works particularly well with mushrooms.

- *Spells.* Add lemon juice or lemon peel to spells to increase their brightness and vibrancy.

Salt to Protect

Salt is used for grounding, protection, and purification. It was always treated as sacred by our ancestors and was once the main preservative of foods. Here are just a few ideas ideas on how to use it in your home:

- *Candles.* Prevent candles from dripping when burning down by soaking them in a strong salt-water mix for a couple of hours.

- *Eggs.* Add a couple of teaspoons of salt to a cup of water, then drop in an egg to test its freshness. If it's fresh, it will sink to the bottom; if it's not, it will float to the top. This is because as an egg gets older, the amount of air inside it increases, making it float.

- *Disinfectant.* Soak cloths and sponges in a salt-water solution to disinfect them.

- *Bee stings.* Treat a bee sting with a paste of salt and water to reduce inflammation and pain.

- *Soot.* Throw salt on your open fire. As it burns, it will help loosen any soot in the chimney.

- *Milk.* Add a pinch of salt to a carton of milk to keep it fresher longer.

- *Coffee.* Add a pinch of salt to coffee to make it taste less bitter.

- *Stains.* Use a salt paste to remove blood, wine, and perspiration stains.

- *Exfoliator.* Use a mixture of salt and olive oil as a great exfoliator.

- *Pests.* Sprinkle salt around the base of your plant pots to deter slugs and snails.

- *Protection.* Sprinkle salt around the outside of your home and wash your front door frame with salt water to provide protection.

- *Negativity.* Place a dish of salt on your table to absorb any negativity from conversations.

Magical Powder

Baking soda, or bicarbonate of soda, is one of the things you should never be without at home. It's so useful for so many tasks that it seems to have a magic of its own. Here are some tips for using this magical white powder:

- *Deodorant.* Try it as an underarm deodorant by applying it with a powder puff.

- *Baths.* Add a cup to bathwater to soften your skin.

- *Bites and burns.* Mix to a paste with water and apply to relieve itching from insect bites and sunburn pain.

- *Odors.* Remove strong odors from your hands by rubbing them with baking soda and water.

- *Flowers.* Keep cut flowers fresh longer by adding a teaspoon to the water in the vase.

- *The fridge.* Place some in the fridge in a small tub or half a lemon shell to absorb odors.

- *Foot odor.* Sprinkle it into your boots and shoes to eliminate pongy foot odor.

- *Pests.* Scatter it around your vegetable beds to prevent bunnies from eating your veggies.

- *Litter box.* Sprinkle it onto your cat's litter box to absorb the bad odor.

- *Carpets.* Clean and freshen carpets and upholstery by sprinkling it over them and gently brushing it in. Leave for an hour or overnight, then vacuum to remove.

- *Strewing.* Use as a strewing blessing for your home. Just mix the powder with flowers and petals or a few drops of essential oil and strew around the floor. You can say something like: "I ask for blessings on this place."

CAMOUFLAGING YOUR MAGIC

Talking of dishes of salt to absorb any negativity brings to mind the horror I saw on a friend's face the first time she walked into my home and was presented with my newly set-up altar. There stood my cauldron, smoke swirling from the incense lit within. Surrounding it were candles, a bell, and a pentacle tile. You could almost see the words "Satan worshipper" fall from her mouth, although she actually said nothing. Suffice it to say that we didn't remain friends for very long. I have a feeling she was a bit wary of me after that, to say the least!

I learned a very valuable lesson that day—one that will always stay with me. It stands to reason that not everyone thinks alike. And, although close family and friends may be very accepting of who you are and whatever your beliefs may be, people don't necessarily want to walk into your home and have witchy stuff under their noses at every turn. So what do you do when dear old granny comes for a cuppa or Mrs. Nosey drops in from next door?

I have found that, for me, the best way to practice what I believe is to make it part of everything I do. So I use everything around me to do this. For example, that dish of salt is just a dish of salt to everyone else—only you need to know its true purpose. You can apply this to everything around your home, and—let's be honest—it's a whole lot cheaper than going out and buying expensive equipment.

Think about what you can use—bowls of water and salt, a saucepan for a cauldron (after all, that's what a cauldron is). A wooden spoon is your wand in the kitchen; bunches of herbs are your spells. Incense and candles are something most of us use anyway; jars of oils and pastes in the bathroom are part of the norm. My pestle and mortar is a bowl and a small rolling pin; my Book of Shadows is kept with my recipe books. I do have a formal altar set up in my bedroom now, and it is a wonderful place to carry out rituals and spells. But it's the everyday things in my home that hold the magic for me, because I use them for making magic every day!

Think about what you use all the time at home and what it really means to you. It's amazing how you can be surrounded by all that equipment and dear old granny need never know—except for that crystal pentacle thing hanging in the front window. I wonder if anyone's noticed that?

WITCHY WAYS TO CELEBRATE MARCH

Here are some things you can do to celebrate the rebirth we all experience in March:

- Decorate your home and altar with displays of eggs—colored and natural—in baskets and bowls. Bring in yellow flowers—daffodils, celandines, and dandelions.

- Set long-term spells for the future that will grow and gain power as the light increases and the Wheel turns.

- Start the gardening year and celebrate the earth by planting seeds, even just some mustard and cress on your windowsill.

- Spring clean yourself and your home by using cleansing herbs in your cleaning rituals. Rosemary is wonderful for this. And clean in a clockwise direction to imbue your work with positivity.

- Celebrate the March winds by working with the air element for spells. Burn incense or just get outside and throw your arms to the winds!

March Folklore

"When March comes in like a lion, it goes out like a lamb."

"A dry March and a wet May bring barns and bays with corn and hay."

"As it rains in March, so it rains in June."

"March winds and April showers bring forth May flowers."

Chapter Two

April

Umbrellas and rainy showers
It's the month for elemental powers.
The buds are forming on the trees,
It will soon be time for busy bees!

Foods at Their Best in April

Fruits and Vegetables

broccoli, carrots, cucumber, cabbages, cauliflower, Jersey royal, leeks, lettuces, mint, new potatoes, purple sprouting broccoli, radishes, rhubarb, rocket, rosemary, spring greens, sea kale, salsify, spinach, sorrel, spring onions, watercress

Seafood

cockles, crab, eel, halibut, John Dory, lobster, lemon sole, mackerel, mussels, oysters, salmon, sardines, sea bass, sea trout, whelks, winkles

Wild Foods

bistort, chickweed, dandelion (leaves, buds, flowers), daisy, hawthorn leaves, hop shoots, hogweed, nettles, St. George's mushrooms, sea beet, tansy leaves, morel mushrooms, violet, wood pigeon, wild garlic

April Correspondences

- *Festival:* Beltane Eve, May Day Eve. Symbols include blossom, May baskets, honey, and garlands.

- *Moon name:* Pink Moon. Flowers start to appear, including wild ground phlox. Other names include Sprouting Grass Moon, Egg Moon, Seed Moon, and Awakening Moon.

- *Astrological signs:* Aries, March 21–April 20; Taurus, April 21–May 20.

- *Birthstones:* Diamond and rock crystal.

- *Nature spirits:* All plant fairies.

- *Animals:* Toads, frogs, squirrels, and bees.

- *Birds:* Wood pigeon and cuckoo.

- *Trees:* Ash and hazel.

- *Flowers:* Daisy, dandelion, bluebell, primrose, and comfrey.

- *Herbs:* Basil, chives, and comfrey.

- *Scents:* Blossoms, grass, and daisy.

- *Colors:* Pale yellow, pinks, and violets.

- *Goddess:* Rhiannon.

- *Powers:* Creative energy, joy, and confidence.

- *Other:* April Fool's Day, Easter (depending on the date), Primrose Day, St. George's Day (England).

April showers bring May flowers, or so they say. April is definitely one of those months when you never know what you're going to get, but you can almost guarantee you will have showers—and lots of them! Some years, you will be blessed with warm spring sunshine and only the odd rain cloud. Most years, however, you will be deluged by a torrent of never-ending rain and winds. It is really not the month to be gliding around in a cloak; best be thinking of a raincoat and brolly. We in Britain are obsessed with the weather—which stands to reason, I guess, as we have so much of it.

My birthday is in April, so I have a fondness for this month—and all its flaws. I think that birthdays should be celebrated by the mum, don't you? After all, she's the one who did all the work; she should at least get some flowers each year in honor of the stretch marks and baggy bits that came from creating the birthday boy or girl. I have a wonderfully clear memory of one of my birthdays—my eleventh—when we had to clear the path of snow so we could get out of the house. Well, I say "we" cleared the path, but in reality, I probably threw snowballs while my brother Michael, Mr. Silent and Sulky, did all the work. Thankfully, we don't get snow that often in April, but we are still regularly caught out by sharp nighttime frosts and foggy mornings. So gardeners, beware of your precious seedling babies.

Out and about in nature, the stars of the show are (drumroll) the trees, as they wake up from their winter slumber. Hurrah! In April, they grace themselves in all their green finery, their leaves uncurling on every branch and changing our world from the gray-brown of winter to dazzling shades of fresh new life. Doesn't the world seem so much brighter when leaves clothe the trees? Ummm, not really surprising, I guess. I know I, for one, look better with my clothes on!

In April, I usually make my first trip of the year into the woods. The new leaves give a perfect dappled canopy to the other stars of this month's show—the bluebells. If there is any more gobsmacking sight than a carpet of bluebells in an English wood in April, I have yet to find it. From around the third week of April, this spectacular blue carpet with its heady fragrance pulls not only me, but so many people who don't really like the great outdoors into the woods to trample through the inevitable slippery mud. Wellies are essential here, as I have found that trainers just do not cut it when you want to stand and stare at this beautiful spectacle. The bluebells of April have a special meaning for my family, as my mum loved them and always said that she wanted to be scattered in them when she passed. And so she was. Now, the sight of every bluebell reminds me of her. So much better than an old gray stone, don't you think?

If you do make it to the woods, be on the lookout for some of the other beauties of April as well—wood anemones with their star-like white flowers, wood sorrel, woodruff, and wild garlic, which you will probably find with your nose before you see it. This pungent wild plant, otherwise known as ramsons, is one of the best seasonal treats you can gather. It can be used in the same way as normal garlic, but I love to use the leaves themselves, just as they are.

Green Man Greens (serves 4)

Here is a fresh vibrant recipe that celebrates all things green. It's simple, quick, and easy to make. But best of all, it uses that very seasonal wild garlic while it's at its best.

Ingredients

1 sweetheart cabbage, finely shredded

1 large leek, finely sliced

1 large handful of wild garlic leaves, washed

1 large handful of dandelion leaves, washed

50 g./1.5 oz. butter

Salt and pepper

Method

1. In a large saucepan over medium heat, mix the butter and a good seasoning of salt and pepper. Melt the butter and seasoning gently together until foamy, but not colored.

2. Add the shredded cabbage and sliced leek to the pan with a tablespoon of hot water and stir well. Cover and steam for 3–4 minutes, stirring occasionally.

3. When the cabbage and leeks are just softened, add the wild garlic and dandelion leaves to the pan.

4. Stir through for a minute, until the leaves are just wilted.

5. Tip into a warm serving bowl and scatter with wild garlic flowers or dandelion petals.

This festival of green goes wonderfully with fish, or serve it simply with a poached egg on the top. Mix any leftovers with mashed potato for a gorgeous bubble and squeak.

THE ELEMEПT OF WATER

Water is the life-blood of our existence, even though it is something we probably don't think about that much. Its magical properties are used by us in so many ways each day, and we don't even notice. Washing, cleaning, cooking, bathing—these can all be magical rituals of transformation and purification that involve the element of water. Even the little monsters running round with their water pistols are celebrating the feeling that water gives us. How many of us revel in that feeling of freedom we get when swimming, with our body weight supported in this magical fluid? We come from a watery womb and so are connected strongly to this element from our very beginning.

In a magical circle, the water element sits in the west. (I remember it by the W for water and for west). It is a feminine element and represents your emotions. Water is the element you should turn to for healing and purifying anything—from yourself to your tools. Oceans, seas, lakes, rivers, streams, springs, and even puddles all have the elemental water force that draw us to them. My favorite place in the world is Swallowhead Spring, a magical little spring that feeds into the clear cool River Kennett, across from the magnificent Silbury Hill and near West Kennett Longbarrow.

You can use this wonderful element for any spell, but here is one I love to do because of the simple and powerful way it uses the emotional healing and purification connection of water. It's a great spell for children to do, because they can see their worries actually flow away with the water.

Let Go Water Spell

You will need:

- A piece of paper

- A pen

- A bay leaf

- A stick—willow if you can find it, as it has an association with water; if not, any stick will do the job

- A long piece of grass/reed, or thread

Sit quietly for a time in the comfort of your home. Think carefully about anything emotional you want to let go of in your life. It may be anger, guilt, fear, or worry—anything that you need to release to move on with your life. If you are doing this for a child, keep things simple. Is the child worried about anything? Or angry?

When you're ready, write down on your piece of paper the thing you wish to let go. Keep your words simple and concise—for example: "I let go of guilt," or "I let go of anger." Sometimes children can't put things into words, so it may help if you encourage them to draw how they feel.

When you have written down what you want to release, place the bay leaf on top of the piece of paper to add extra power to your wishes. Place the stick on top of the paper and bay leaf, then roll the paper and leaf around the stick. Tie the paper roll into position with the long grass/reed or thread. As you do this, say something simple like:

I bind this spell, so mote it be!

Take the spell that you created and travel to your chosen body of water. If you can, walk to a river and spend the time thinking of what you are letting go. If you have to drive there, spend a few minutes when you arrive to think of what you have written.

At the river or the sea, hold your spell in your cupped hands and focus on letting go. Listen to the sound of the water and know that it is there to help wash away any negativity that you ask it to. When you're ready, release your spell to the river or the sea. As you release it, say something like:

I release these emotions, with thanks so mote it be!

Watch as the river or sea carries away your wish. Know that it will recycle any negativity into positivity. As your spell is carried away, close your eyes and know that you have been relieved of these emotions—that the element of water has taken them from you. Feel the lightness as your burden lifts. If you're doing this with a child, have them shout "go" or "goodbye" when they release the spell. Make it a joyous act.

Back at home, place a small dish of water on your altar and light a candle of thanks to this cleansing element. If you can't get to a river or the sea, try this spell with a symbolic bowl of water at home. Once you've released your spell to the water in the bowl, take it outside and pour both the water and the spell onto the earth, then bury your spell for the earth and water to recycle.

I believe that we should try to think of water and the part it plays in our lives every day. Bringing it into our consciousness really helps us use water as the vital fluid it is. And that's magical.

BALANCING FAMILY AND MAGIC

Balancing your family life with your magical life can be tough, even for the most organized of people. For normal, try-to-get-through-the-day-without-any-disasters kind of people like myself, trying to achieve a balance between the magical and the day-to-day can sometimes seem impossible. For me, magic isn't something that should be viewed as a separate entity; it can and should be seen as an everyday thing.

Now, I don't mean that we should all be going about our daily lives with a wand tucked under one arm, chanting rituals through the latest school play, or wandering around the local park with a spell book in one hand and a bag of yummy nettles in the other. More likely (if you are lucky), you will be trudging along with a bag of yummy nettles in one hand while you use the other to control a hyperactive child and a mischievous dog trying to get off the lead and play with some other dog! Magical practices shouldn't be kept just for ritual purposes. In this modern world, it is more important than ever to embrace the magic of everyday life and connect with others out there who do the same thing. I, for one, know that my world would certainly be duller without it.

Finding a balance between life and magic can take some practice, however. It's sometimes really hard to remember things like "harm none" when frustration boils up at the supermarket checkout. Be honest now—how many loving and kind thoughts pass through your head when you're stuck in a traffic jam and you're late? Or when your darling little toddler creates his or her most recent masterpiece all over your cream carpet and walls? Learning how to create balance in your own mind can help you live your life magically. On the other hand, I feel it's really important to remember that we are human; we are not perfect, nor is anyone else! You will always find times and situations when balance goes out the window and when, no matter how magically you try to live each day, you find yourself banging your head against the nearest brick wall. Life is just like that.

Beginnings and Endings

So how can you start to create a balance in your mind that gives you a fighting chance of living magically? Well, for me, it's about beginnings and endings. The start of each new day practically screams "new start"—the sun is rising and the birds are singing. Balance for the day can come as a simple affirmation to yourself as you get dressed or have a shower. Breakfast can be a balanced affair with harmonious foods and a simple ritual. But things are rarely that simple, are they? There are children to drag out of bed and send to school, pets to be fed and walked, and chores to do—all before you even have the chance to think. It is not easy getting off to a good start each day, so you have to be realistic about what you can achieve.

The best way I have found to start each day with balance in mind is to write down an affirmation and prop it up on my bedside cabinet. I also have another one pinned up in the bathroom. This way, as I reach for man's most hated machine— the alarm clock—the first thing I see is something balanced. When I stumble bleary-eyed into the bathroom to brush my teeth—there it is again, just in case my everyday mind has already forgotten what the first one said!

Affirmations are, quite simply, phrases that you can say each day as positive affirmative statements. Say them often enough and they become ingrained in your mind—a bit like retraining for your brain, shoving in a positive to override a negative. Think carefully about what you want to see every morning to help you face the day, and try to focus on bringing balance. My morning affirmation currently reads:

I will bring my craft into all I do today,
With balance in an old and new way.

Try to make sure you place your affirmation somewhere where you will see it every morning. And if you find that, after a while, you stop noticing it, change the location. Think about what words work for you; keep them simple and positive. During the day, try to bring your affirmation to mind as often as possible. Soon you will find that, as you do, you will take on more and more daily tasks with magic in your mind—everything from the dusting to making dinner. It's amazing the difference it can make. I mean, it's not as if we forget our magic; it just sometimes slips out of our minds in the middle of a heated telephone call.

Affirmations also work well at the end of the day. But for me, the end of the day is about recognizing the night and acknowledging the balance of light and dark—the sun and the moon and the different energies they lend to us, if we just notice that they're there. The night comes to slow us down, allowing us to rest from the day-to-day world. It gives us time to reflect and plan the following day. Well, that's the theory anyway. We no longer live by the light as our ancestors did; electricity allows us to work as much in the evening as during the day. What with dinners to be made, kids' bedtimes to see to, and maybe even an occasional conversation with your poor neglected other half, evenings seem to take on a life of their own.

Evening is the time of day when we can perhaps take some time for ourselves—and most of us in the modern world turn on the computer to do it. Time online has become our new social life—a time when we access the world and meet new friends. We answer emails and play games that allow our brains to switch off for a bit. Thank goodness for that, I say. But time online also gives us a valuable opportunity to converse with like-minded people. It offers a great time to find balance between your life and your magic. Seek out information through your computer screen—the world is at your fingertips. Find sites that you relate to and interact with them. We don't have gatherings of people anymore to create magic and share knowledge, but we can find the same opportunities with a few clicks of a mouse.

If you do go online in the evening, whether to work or to play games, try giving yourself some time to nurture your craft. Learn about an herb you may have used that day or comment on a post you may have seen. Become part of the magical world that connects us to each other across the seas in a matter of moments. I have met some amazingly wonderful people through the Hedgewitch Cooks website. Some of them I have gone on to meet personally; some of them I have come to consider my online family. I love to hear how they connect with magic and the world around them. This is something I would never get the chance to do without access to the World Wide Web. Living a largely solitary life doesn't mean that you have to be lonely! By making some time to be with others, even virtually, you can create a balance in your life. Always remember Internet safety, however. Never give out personal information—and if in doubt, bail out. Trust your own instincts; if it doesn't feel right, it probably isn't.

Mother Nature

There is one thing I would like to add here about finding balance—probably the most important thing of all. And it has to do with Mother Nature. She is the champion at balancing the realities of everyday life and magic, so we should all take some time every day to learn from her. Make sure you get to see something of her every day—take a walk with the dog, or walk to the school, or just stand and look at the trees or the plants in your garden. Even in the middle of the city, Mother Nature can be seen through the cracks in the pavements and walls. Look for her each and every day; there is always something new to notice. If you do spend some of your evening online, try to make the last thing you do before you go to bed something that physically connects you to the world, the universe you live in, and Mother Nature.

For me, the best way to connect with the night, with the moon and the stars, is to take time to acknowledge that they are there. You can just stand outside for a few minutes and take in the magic that's around you. Or, if you can't get out, open your curtains and stand in a darkened room to take in the night through your window. Take this time for a few deep breaths; concentrate on the stillness of the night and how different it is from the hustle and bustle of the day. Listen to the sounds of Mother Nature at night—the wind blowing and the rain falling. Feel yourself being connected with the earth, grounded within its space and time. You and all that you do are part of it all. Feel that sense of belonging to something, of being an essential part of the whole. You may say some simple words like:

I am in balance with the world; I am grounded to her.

Once you have made this part of your nighttime routine, you will never look back. There is something so affirming about connecting with the outside world just before you curl up in your bed. And I'll bet you sleep better, too.

Balance takes practice. If you are just discovering your path, it stands to reason that you will throw yourself into everything that screams magic. But with time and experience, a gentler way of magic unfolds. No one can live a life of magic without interruption from the normality of everyday life. But with time and knowledge, a harmonious joining of the two will happen within you and you will find that you approach most tasks with magic in your heart and mind. That's when you will know that you've found balance.

Keeping Things Affordable

These days, with a wealth of online shops available to us, it seems there isn't anything that you can't buy anymore. Now, I am definitely not a clothes-shopping girl—I actually dread it—but I am a sucker for a mystical shop. At least once a year, daughter number one and I make the journey from Wiltshire down the road to magical Glastonbury in Somerset. There, in the land of Avalon, we can immerse ourselves in all things witchy. The high street is lined with gorgeous shops selling everything from wands to books to crystals. It is definitely a real treat to wander around and look at all those tempting goodies—an amazing day out for the soul and a disaster waiting to happen for my purse! Although I have to be honest and say that we never come away from Glastonbury without a shopping bag, I really believe that you don't need to spend anything much to acquire your magical tools. The basics of Hedgewitchery always come from inside you and from the hedgerow. However, sometimes, when you want to do things a little more formally for a ritual or Sabbat, it is nice to have a magical tool kit to dip into. So here are some purse-friendly ideas you can use for the basics.

Wand

Wands are used as an extension of your hands to direct energy into a spell or ritual. In the kitchen, your wand is your wooden spoon and you can use it to stir magic into what you're creating. If you wish to own an actual wand, look to Mother Nature as a source. Before you go out, take a few minutes to focus on finding your wand, and ask that you be given help to find it. Out you go and keep your eyes open. Look for a fallen branch that is approximately the length of your arm from elbow to wrist; it doesn't have to be exact. You will know when you find the right one.

It doesn't matter what kind of wood your wand is, but if you know what kind of wand you have found, it can be fun to research the meaning of that tree. Often, the wand you find has been given to you for a reason, and it will lend you the power you need.

Once you've found your wand, you can adorn it however you like—perhaps with carvings or crystals or ribbons—and shine it up with olive oil. Get to know your wand and you will have many years of a beautiful magical relationship together!

Athame

An athame is a knife or dagger that is used in ceremonies and rituals. But unlike a normal kitchen knife, which should always be sharp, the athame should always be blunt, because it is only used for cutting one thing—a hand-fasting cake. Now, if you need a sharp knife to cut your hand-fasting cake, it is probably inedible!

Like your wand, your athame is used mainly to direct energy and to carve symbols and words onto candles. You can create your own athame by blunting a kitchen knife you already own on a piece of stone. Or, if you can, have a look in the charity or junk shops for a wooden-handled knife. You can decorate the wooden handle just as you decorated your wand.

Offering Bowl

This can be a really useful item to set aside as a magical tool. An offering bowl is something you should always use when you create magic. If you're in the kitchen, place a spoonful of the foods you make in the bowl. If your bowl is set on an altar, you can offer anything from flowers to food in it.

My offering bowl is an essential element of what I do, so I use a pretty bowl I picked up at a yard sale. You can use any bowl you like, so root around in your cupboards (or anyone else's) and find one that feels right to you. Keep it solely for magical use, however—no serving up pudding in it. Kind of defeats the purpose!

Candles

I think all of us who follow a magical path use candles practically every day. If you look in my house, you might think that you need to call the local fire brigade because of the number of flickering flames. But candles can be expensive. You can buy a candle-making kit and make your own, but I am not that crafty and the whole candle-making process scares the hell out of me. It looks far too much like a science lesson for my liking.

Most of the candles that I use are either birthday candles or white tea lights that can be picked up fairly inexpensively at the supermarket. It's worth looking online too, especially for votives and larger candles. You can get some great deals on the online auction sites.

Incense and Essential Oils

Incense is an easy one to keep affordable, because incense is relatively cheap anyway if you buy it in stick or cone form. If, however, you want to use loose incense, this can get more costly because it often contains resins as well as herbs. Try making your own incense by using dried herbs or flowers, or look online for one base resin to start with. I like frankincense, because it works with most things.

Another way to get the aromas you need is by using essential oils. Although the bottles these oils come in are small and it can cost quite a bit for a good-quality oil, they last for ages. When you use a burner, you only need a couple of drops of oil in water for the scent to fill the air. And the oils are easy to blend together too, so get creative!

Pentacle

A pentacle is a five-pointed star with one point facing up. It can be depicted with or without a circle around it and is used mainly as a focus or symbol of the craft. Try making your own with modeling clay, or simply draw one on a piece of paper. I painted my pentacle onto a plain ceramic tile. A nice way to make a natural pentacle is to dry out a slice of apple that has been cut width-wise and, voilá, you have your own natural focus point!

Eggs and Eggshells

Now I want to share with you some great tips for using eggshells. And it only makes sense to jump to the kitchen to cook something with eggs first. This recipe is wonderful for spring, as eggs represent life itself.

Enchanted Eggs (serves 4)

Ingredients

4 large tomatoes

4 portions of bacon or Parma ham

4 eggs

8 basil leaves

A splash of oil

Salt and pepper

Tabasco sauce

Method

1. Preheat the oven to 180°C/350°F.

2. Remove the tops of the tomatoes and scoop out the seeds. Turn upside down on a plate to drain.

3. Smear the tomatoes with a little oil and season well with salt and pepper.

4. Wrap each tomato with a piece of bacon or Parma ham and secure with a toothpick.

5. Place 2 basil leaves in each tomato and place on a tray. Pop in the oven for 15 minutes, or until the tomatoes start to soften and the bacon begins to crisp.

6. After 15 minutes, remove the tomatoes from the oven.

7. Break an egg into each tomato, saying:

> *Enchanted egg, provide for me*
> *The knowledge of life inside.*
> *May my eyes and heart be open*
> *To the power that you provide!*

1. Top each egg with a splash of Tabasco and return to the oven for approx. 5 minutes, or until the egg is cooked but the yolk is still runny.

1. Serve with toast soldiers (toast cut into strips) for breakfast or brunch, or with a big herb salad and a large glass of wine for a light lunch in the garden. You can adapt this recipe by adding cheese or a different herb—thyme works really well.

Now that you've enchanted some eggs, you should have some eggshells to use. What do you do with your eggshells? Compost them? Well, as great as they are in the compost, why not try to put them to good use in some other ways? Here are some top uses for eggshells:

- *Bandages.* Use that slippery membrane inside the shell as a natural bandage over small cuts and blisters. It really does work!

- *Coffee.* Add crushed shells to your fresh coffee to make it less bitter.

- *Pests.* Sprinkle crushed shells around your pots and garden plants to deter slugs and snails from making that juicy shoot their next meal.

- *Tomatoes.* Give your tomatoes a calcium boost and help prevent blossom rot by adding crushed eggshell to the planting hole for your plants.

- *Starter pots.* Use eggshell halves as starter pots for seedlings. Just fill with a little compost and plant your seeds, then plant outside when they are big enough—just avoid disturbing the roots. You can keep the shells upright while the shoots grow by using the carton the eggs came in.

- *Blender blades.* Keep some shells in the freezer and use them to clean and sharpen your blender blades. Simply put the frozen shells and some water into the blender and blend! Pour the mixture onto your compost heap when you are done.

- *Calcium vinegar.* Make calcium vinegar by adding calcium-rich herbs (nettles, dock, etc.) and one clean eggshell to a jar full of apple-cider vinegar. Leave the mixture to infuse for around six weeks, then strain and decant. This will give you a wonderful mineral-rich vinegar to use in place of an ordinary one to give added boost to your salads and dishes.

- *Vases.* Put crushed eggshells in a tall glass or vase with soapy water and swirl it around to clean hard-to-reach spots at the bottom.

- *Whitener.* Make a homemade whitener sachet for your laundry by putting a handful of clean and broken eggshells and 2 slices of lemon in a cheesecloth bag. Place this in with your clothes when you wash them to prevent the soap deposits that sometimes turn your white clothes gray.

- *Mosaics.* Wash the shells and break them into medium-sized pieces. Color them and use them to create homemade mosaics—a wonderful project for bored little hands!

BELTANE

Before we jump into chapter 3, a note on Beltane. Beltane Eve occurs on the magical night when April fades into May. It is the time when fair maidens and handsome young men disappear into the forest to—well, let's just say enjoy themselves! It is the time when fertility is at its height, a time for another celebration. So on April 30, grab your other half if you have one and go frolicking out in the woods—that is, if you can find a babysitter, it's not raining or cold, and you have the energy. On second thought, maybe a cuppa in front of the telly?

WITCHY WAYS TO CELEBRATE APRIL

- Decorate your home and altar with garlands of flowers and ribbons in beautiful pastel shades.

- Make a simple May pole centerpiece from a foraged stick and some ribbons. Decorate it with moss and flowers and use it as your focus.

- Connect with the element of water for your spells. Visit a river or stream and have a pretty bowl of water out in your home.

- Celebrate all live reproduction by combining ingredients in your cooking. April is an ideal month for fertility spells and rituals.

- Welcome the returning birds by setting up a bird feeder in your garden.

April Folklore

"April showers bring May flowers."

"If early April is foggy, then rain in June will make lanes boggy!"

"When April blows its horn, 'tis good for hay and corn."

"April wet, good wheat."

"Till April's dead, change not a thread."

Chapter Three

MAY

This is the time for joy and play
The hedgerows are full with such a display.
Make merry and embrace the light
Dance in the greenwood on Beltane night!

Foods at Their Best in May

Fruit and Vegetables

British asparagus, broad beans, broccoli, chicory, cauliflower, cucumber, fennel, Jersey royal, kohlrabi, mint, new potatoes, nasturtium (flowers and leaves), radishes, rocket, sorrel, spring onions, rhubarb, watercress

Seafood

cockles, coley, cod, crab, halibut, herring, John Dory, lemon sole, lobster, mackerel, sea bass, salmon, sea trout, pollack, plaice, salmon, sardines, winkles, whelks

Wild Food

borage flowers, carrageen, dandelion, daisy, elderflowers, marsh samphire, nettles, plantain, sorrel, sea purslane, wild garlic, wild mint, wood pigeon

May Correspondences

- *Festival*: Beltane, May Day. Symbols include the May pole, boughs of flowers, and fires.

- *Moon name*: Flower Moon. Flowers come into full bloom and the corn is ready to be planted. Other names include Grass Moon, Milk Moon, Hare Moon, and Corn Planting Moon.

- *Astrological signs*: Taurus, April 21–May 20; Gemini, May 21–June 20.

- *Birthstones*: Emerald and agate.

- *Nature spirits*: Tree fairies and spirits.

- *Animals*: All cats, butterflies, and foxes.

- *Birds*: Swallow, dove, and swift.

- *Trees*: Hawthorn, apple, and elder.

- *Flowers*: All tree blossoms, foxglove, and lilac.

- *Herbs*: St. John's wort, chamomile, flowering thyme, elderflower, and yarrow.

- *Scents*: Rose, frankincense, honeysuckle, lilac, and jasmine.

- *Colors*: Pink, apricot, and green.

- *Goddess*: Diana.

- *Powers*: Love, fertility, and joy—the expressive energy of life's forces.

- *Other*: May Day, Labor Day, Oak Apple Day.

So did you go frolicking last night? No? He he he, me neither—too cold and uncomfortable for a midlife witch. I think I'll leave all that cavorting to you youngsters out there! But celebrating Beltane, well that's a completely different thing. I think of all the festivals (Sabbats) that we celebrate throughout the Wheel of the Year, Beltane is my favorite. It actually begins at moonrise on May Eve (April 30) and celebrates the turning out of livestock into the pastures. The cattle were driven through fires to protect them from all ills—a dangerous heart-in-the-mouth procedure if you ask me! Fires are still a strong symbol of Beltane, with hilltop fires still lit to symbolize the sun as it gains strength.

English village communities raised the May pole to celebrate this wonderful fire festival, and the May pole was the focal point of the day. All the people of the village emerged on May Day morn to dance around this rather saucy phallic symbol festooned with flowers and ribbons to weave the good luck into their lives. Both women and men decorated themselves with flowers and garlands and brought May blossoms into their homes to ensure good luck. In my home, my mum used to say that May blossoms should not be brought into the house except on May Day, and I still hold to that!

The May Day festival is all about passion—all about the union of man and woman, about fertility and vigor and deep love. It's the time when we celebrate the Goddess and the Green Man creating life together, she in her maiden aspect and he in the role of passionate and virile young man. Oh, I say!

Fertility is all around us in nature; the time of reproduction is here! Now, just because we aren't all out cavorting in the grass (although even married men and women used to take off their wedding rings and leave their vows at home for the day) doesn't mean we can't celebrate this amazing turn of the Wheel. Oh no! Traditionally, people braided their hair, jumped through a fire, danced around the May pole, and hand-fasted (got married), committing themselves to one another. In our modern world, all these wonderful things aren't necessarily practical—although if you have the time and energy, don't let anyone stop you! Instead, why not try a simple walk on May Day morning and plan for something you can all do together. I propose a feast—after all, what is a party without one? And what better way to kick off any party than to have something sweet and yummy?

Elderflower Pancakes (serves 6)

Ingredients

110 g./2 oz. plain/all-purpose flour, sifted

A pinch of salt

2 eggs

200 ml./6.5 oz. milk mixed with 75 ml./2.5 oz. water

50 g./1.5 oz. butter

2 full heads of just-opened elderflowers, washed

and with the flowers stripped with a fork

Lemon and icing sugar to serve

Method

1. Sift the flour and salt together in a mixing bowl.

2. Make a well in the center of the flour and break in the eggs. Whisk together.

3. Gradually add the milk-and-water mixture. Keep whisking until all the liquid has been added and the batter is smooth.

4. Add the elderflowers, stirring gently and reserving a few for the end.

5. Melt the butter in a saucepan. Add 2 tbsp. into the batter and mix, then pour the rest into a separate bowl.

6. Place a small frying pan or crêpe pan over a medium heat until very hot. Using a ladle, add some batter to the pan and swirl around until the bottom of the pan is thinly coated. Cook on each side for a minute or so, or until golden.

1. To serve, sprinkle each pancake with the remaining elderflowers, lemon juice, and icing sugar.

These wonderful crêpes, like pancakes, are fragrant and sweet. They keep beautifully if you layer them between sheets of waxed paper and freeze. Try making a simple elderflower syrup with elderflower heads, sugar, and water to drizzle over them. What better way to celebrate Beltane?

The Goddess and God in Everyday Life

Celebrating the Goddess and God is something we do through festivals as the Wheel turns through the year. But have you really thought about who these figures are that we celebrate and how they relate to us and our everyday world?

It is easy for me to connect with the Goddess every day, because I feel she is all around me. She is Mother Earth. In her triple aspect, she is Maiden, Mother, and Crone. Women all go through these stages throughout our lives in the way that Mother Nature goes through them in a year. That is not to say that you can't be a maiden in your eighties or a crone in your twenties. But, on the whole, we each have within us the triple aspect that follows the cycles as nature does. In our maiden aspect, we go through adolescence and are at our most fertile. In our mother aspect, we carry, give birth to, and care for children. In our crone aspect, after fertility has ended, we become guides—wise and all-knowing (well, that's the idea anyway!).

To truly connect with the Goddess, however, you don't have to be at any particular age or even be a female. This connection is all about feeling the rhythms of the world around you. Look inside yourself, as well as outside in the world. Do you feel inside what is reflected outside? Do you feel a spring in your step in the spring? A relaxed contentment in the summer? An inward drawing of the curtains in the winter? Do you feel aspiration and hope? Sadness and fear? This is your connection to the Goddess—the life blood of the world—and you are a part of it.

The Goddess is you and you are the Goddess. There is no separation between the two, so there is no need to seek her. She is already there within you! She represents your soul; she is the heartbeat and mind of your self and all that is around you. The way to connect with her is just to listen to what's going on inside yourself and to recognize the patterns and cycles as you live your everyday life. Nurture the Goddess within you by simply thinking of her; make her happy, and be together.

You can't nurture a relationship with the Goddess without loving yourself, so when you spend time taking care of yourself, you are taking care of her too. Try a simple affirmation every day in front of the mirror. Say something simple like:

I nurture myself and so the Goddess, today and always.

When you remember her, you make her part of your everyday life and you begin to see her in all things. It's as if you remove a blindfold and suddenly have 20/20 vision. Call on her when you cast your spells and do your rituals. She is always there to lend you her strength; her gift to you is life itself.

The God is celebrated in relation to the Goddess, and—let's be honest—there can be no creation without both! The God is known by many names—Herne, Pan, Cernunnos, Lord of the Wildwood, or the Green Man. He is so much more than simply the partner of the Goddess, however. He is the power and driving force behind all life. All wild animals represent the God, hence the description "horned God." He can be found as the sun that sets and rises in a never-ending cycle, and as the passions and fire in both animals and you.

The God is a massive part of the Wheel of the Year and is especially linked to the crop cycle—seeds, crops, reaping, dying. He is sovereign over sex, passion, and laughter, and we can connect with him simply through our drive for life every day. He commands us to do something about how we feel; action is the order of the day here! Listen for him in the rustling of the leaves on the trees, in the thunderstorm, or in the mating calls of animals. He, too, is inside you. Feel him every morning giving you the drive to get out of bed and actually do something.

You can use a simple affirmation to connect with the God, too:

I feel the call of the horned God igniting my passion for life.

Hear him inside you, urging you on to do or create. He is there to give you a friendly shove in the right direction and celebrate with you when you achieve.

Green Thumbs

Hopefully, as we go tripping gaily into May, the sunshine and warm breezes that I'm sure I ordered are arriving daily. The threat of frosty nights has now passed and the soil is warming up nicely. So it's time to wake up those green thumbs and hit the garden!

In my garden, May tends to be noisy, with the yowling of cats as they call to each other across the fences. Mine are the main culprits, and I'm sure my neighbors cut their grass just to cover up the song of my feline babies. I can't say I blame them—cat song is an acquired taste.

I do love the proper start of the gardening season, as I'm always brimming over with ideas I came up with during the long winter months. I feel invincible as I rescue the trowel and fork from under the pile of unused pots. Honestly, I never know why I find my tools in such weird places after the winter. I imagine the garden fairies are playing some great practical joke on me.

My favorite things to plant and use are herbs. I never get tired of sowing these tiny unpromising seeds, and reaping and using their wonderful bounty. And it's so easy to create an herb garden and make it different every year! Planning your herb garden can be lots of fun. Think about what you want to use, but also how you want your garden to look. Try making a drawing of your space, however small, and plot out what plants will work where. Create a design that resonates with you. Over the years, I have created a Celtic knot and a pentacle. Once I even designed a witch's broom with different herbs making up the strands of the broom! Parsley, chives, lavender, and rosemary all make amazing edging plants for your design. Then you just fill in the blanks with whatever else you fancy growing. If you want to keep your design, remember to use perennials (plants that come back every year).

Even if you only have space for a few pots or are just making a small garden for your windowsill, remember that soil is the most important part of any garden. Herbs need a rich but free-draining soil. So if your soil is full of clay or is heavy, add some grit to help with the drainage before you plant. Herbs don't need a lot of extra food or care. In fact, the flavor and aroma of herbs improves if they are a little hungry, but don't starve them to death!

The location of your herb garden is key, too. Most herbs are sunbathers and love the light, so if you want the best out of them, give them what they need. No shady corners for these guys! Positioning your garden is just as important for you, because no one wants to trudge across wet, muddy grass for a snipping of chives. So think about easy access and keep your herbs as close to hand as you can. You're more likely to use them in your magic and cooking if you can get to them easily.

So what to plant? There are so many herbs out there to choose from that it can be hard to decide what to use. If you already have an established herb garden, it may be nice to add one or two varieties that are not readily found elsewhere to increase your herbal collection. But if you are creating an herb garden for the first time, it is really worth deciding what you may want to use for cooking and magic, and starting with those. After all, you may have a wealth of recipes that use thyme, for example, but you can't stand the flavor. There's no point in planting what you know you won't use in your cooking. Also, be sure to consider what you will use magically for spells and sachets.

These are some herbs I suggest for a basic herb garden. They are all very useful, both in the kitchen and in magic, and they require very little effort to grow:

Rosemary

Thyme

Sage

Parsley

Lavender

Mint

Chives

Lemon balm

Once you've decided on your design, your soil, your choice of plants, and the location of your garden, it's finally time to plant. The cheapest way to start your herb garden is from seeds and this makes it easy to create your design. But let's create some magic first, to help the seeds on their way.

With a trowel, draw your lines through the soil to the right depth for the seed (it will tell you this on the packet). Then gently sprinkle the seed into each furrow. As you do this, say:

Little seeds burst and grow; let me reap what I now sow.

Gently cover the seeds with soil and water them well. Make sure you protect your lovely new herb patch with something like netting to stop pets and other animals from disturbing the seeds. When you're all done, light a small candle to bless your new patch and leave an offering for the garden fairies to thank them for their help in looking after your seeds. All you have to do then is sit back and wait for your design to sprout.

If you are like me and have limited patience, you can create your herb garden with seedlings or cuttings "borrowed" from a friend's garden. This gives you an instant result and you can still do a little spell to encourage their growth. Dig a hole twice as big as the plant you have. In the bottom of the hole, draw a magical shape with your trowel or finger. I like to use the sun for my herbs. As you do this, say:

Protected above and so below, I will reap just what I sow!

Pour some water into the hole, position your plant, and press it firmly into the soil before watering again. Remember to position your plants with room to grow, not too close to each other. A gap of around six inches is about right for most plants you buy in pots. If you use seedlings, make sure you don't get itchy fingers and start to pick them too early, before they are established—no matter how tempted you may be. Even the toughest-looking specimen needs time to put down roots before getting pulled about—a bit like us, really!

Growing your own food can be so rewarding, and can keep those rising food costs down. I know just how expensive it can be to feed growing kids who change what they will and won't eat daily. My answer is to drag the little angels into the garden with you and give them the task of taking care of an herb or vegetable themselves. I have yet to find a child who doesn't love to watch the progress of a plant from a seed to something they can eat. And not one that I have come across says "I don't like it" when tasting something that they have grown themselves.

This way of introducing children to the wonders of the growing world does only seem to work, however, before they hit puberty. I have very strong memories of a fifteen-year-old daughter being put to work on my garden. Never before have innocent garden plants been subjected to such a blast of negativity and bad language. No plant—even the weeds—should have had to go through that. And don't get me started on the bedroom she was asked to paint either! So trust me, catch them while they're still young and enthusiastic. When you teach children about herbs and plants, you are handing something important on to the next generation—and for that, you can feel rightly smug!

Understanding a little about your herbs will definitely help you get the best from them. For example, if you want to grow something like mint or oregano, it's best to plant them in containers, because they spread everywhere and can take over your other herbs. Think of them as the bullies of the herbal playground. You can always sink the containers into the ground if you don't want to see the pots. Just make sure that the growing tips don't touch the ground or else they'll be off!

Once you've plotted and planned and planted your herb garden, give it some time to put out roots and settle in to its new home before taking anything from it. No plant likes a haircut while it's trying to make its bed. Your herbs will be ready for use soon enough. And once they're growing well, remember that you have them! Use them as much as you can by taking from them sparingly and often. They are designed to be used and will grow and bush out so much faster if you give them an occasional trim. Regeneration is what they do best—a bit like Dr. Who—so put them to good use.

Here are a few tips on what you can do with your herbal bounty in the kitchen:

- *Make a tea.* Experiment with fresh herbal tea by brewing a teaspoon of chopped fresh herb in hot water for around five minutes. The resulting tea will be lighter and fresher than commercial brands and you will get the pure essence of the plant.

- *Dry them out.* Hang up small bunches of herbs in a warm darkish place for two to three weeks, until they are crisp and thoroughly dry. Then store them in air-tight containers or paper bags ready for use. Remember that, when using dried herbs in cooking, you only need around half as much as you would if you were using them fresh. The drying process concentrates the flavor.

- *Freeze them.* Chop your herbs up finely and freeze them in ice cube trays. Once you have little cubes of green, pop them into a freezer bag and store them. They'll be ready for you to add to recipes. Just remember to label your bags clearly. Many's the time I've been confronted by a bag of unknown cubes lurking around in my freezer. It's quite a surprise to get a lemon-balm stuffing with your Sunday roast!

- *Make herb butter.* Add a couple of tablespoons of chopped herbs to approximately 100 grams/3.5 ounces of butter. Season well with salt and pepper and a squeeze of lemon juice. Mix them together thoroughly and shape into a log. Wrap the log in waxed paper, label it, and store it in the fridge or pop it into the freezer. The butter will keep in the fridge for around a week, or in the freezer for up to a month. Experiment with combinations of herbs or keep it simple with a single flavor. When you want an herb, just slice off a piece and melt it on some hot food. This is great on top of grilled meat or fish, or stirred through pasta.

- *Make herb oil or vinegar.* Place sprigs of fresh herbs into a bottle and cover with either vegetable or olive oil, or with vinegar. Allow the mixture to sit and steep for around a month. Use the wonderfully flavored result for cooking, dressings, and for finishing foods. Try experimenting with combinations or adding chilies or garlic to the bottles to produce different flavors. These bottles look so pretty, and they make great gifts!

Medicinal Herbs

The medicinal properties of herbs have been used—well, it seems like forever! Traditionally, our grandparents and those before them turned to herbs as medicine, with wise men and women handing out tinctures and brews for whatever ailed their patients. As things progressed into more modern times, pharmacists used herbs to conjure up cures and to make pills. So is it a shame that modern medicine reaches for synthetic substances rather than the natural remedies our ancestors used?

I believe it's not. Oh no! This modern Hedgewitch thinks we are blessed to live in the times we do, and that every new step on the road to treating and curing disease is amazing. There are so many talented scientists out there doing all they can to cure us of our ailments. I believe they should be celebrated. They are the wise men and women of today and we would be in a right sorry old state if they didn't discover and test and ultimately produce the medicines that they do. I really believe that if our ancestors had access to what we have today, they would grab it with both hands and run with it. But I do think that in a world of modern medicine, there is still a place for using herbs and more natural substances safely in the home.

An extraordinary amount of modern-day medicine still comes from plants and herbs. I don't know of many people who don't reach for an aspirin when in the grip of a crippling headache, and that little pill is based on a substance from the bark of the willow tree. Our ancestors chewed on the bark to relieve pain long before aspirin pills came into use. But I am not a bark chewer, and never will be. Nor do I have time to go off searching for a willow tree every time I have a headache. Do you?

There are a few things you can do at home to help deal with ailments, but honestly, you would need a book written by someone a lot smarter than I am to cover even some of the medicinal uses of herbs. I will say, however, that whatever you read or find out, check it with another source—and then check it again! If you make a mistake using things that you don't know a lot about, it can have serious, even fatal, outcomes. So take no chances. If you are using herbs that are familiar or grown by you, and they are traditionally used in cooking, then you are fairly safe using them to treat ailments at home. Learn all you can before you do, however. Herbs can be potent things. So start slowly with just one or two herbs and become an expert on those first.

Magical Herbs

I probably use herbs more in magic than I do in cooking. The energy and power of each plant seem to speak to me and I put those energies to use in ways I feel is right for that plant at that time. Using herbs magically for cooking and spells can be a wonderful way of connecting with magic every day.

The trick here is to charge your herbs to do exactly what you want them to do. This is a fancy way of saying that you are asking the energy of each plant to work with you to get the outcome you want. It can take some practice to recognize each plant's energy—think of it as trying to tune in a radio frequency perfectly—but in time, you will get the hang of it and be able to tap into the unique properties of the herbs you are using.

Charging Your Herbs and Ingredients

This practice is at the heart of everything I do magically—in the kitchen or around the home. The first task is to select your herb or ingredient and, if you can, try to understand a little about it—where it grows, its traditional uses, and just what it represents to you and yours. Take time to appreciate it fully—how it looks, feels, and smells. What does it say or represent for you?

When you are ready, hold the herb or ingredient between your palms and close your eyes. Focus on what you feel. Do you pick up anything? A vibration or a tingle? You may initially feel nothing, which is completely normal. If that is the case, focus on the texture of what you are holding; focus on the smell.

When you feel in tune with the herb, or when you feel completely relaxed with how it feels in your hands, start to focus on what you want it to do for you. For example, if you want to use or cook with rose petals, you know that they are magically attuned for love, so it makes sense to use them for that purpose. As you hold them, focus on that feeling of love, on their abundantly flowing energy of love. If you are using them for someone or something else, think of that too. Remember, when focusing your intent, always imagine the outcome of your spell. And always imagine abundance and success as already present! When you feel that connection between your own intent and the energy of the plant, you have successfully charged your herb. Practice this as often as you can, whenever you can. And trust in yourself. You know more than you think you do!

When you have charged your herb or ingredient, use it in a way that focuses on what you want from it. If you charged it for love and are making a dish, then stir the love in. If you charged it for peace, then lower the lights and turn off the TV. Remember, magic will only work if you guide it in the right direction. I always charge a sprig of rosemary for daughter number two before an exam. I charge it for memory and insist that she take it with her to smell whenever she needs a boost. So she puts it in her pencil case. I think she thinks I am completely nuts, but she still takes the sprig with her to the exam, so I believe she knows it will work. She just doesn't want to let on; that would be very uncool! And she certainly has the best-smelling pencil case around!

Using herbs magically can be really rewarding. Here are a few ideas on how you can do it:

- *Cook with them.* This is the ultimate way to use the power of herbs magically, because you actually consume your spell.

- *Burn them.* A pinch of a dried herb in a candle flame can be a good base for a spell. Charge your herb first. And make sure you only use a pinch, or those firemen will be out again!

- *Simmer them.* Make a potion on the stove top in a saucepan and simmer it to release the essence of the plants. This can smell wonderful and imbue the air with magic. The downside? Get the wrong combination and your simmering potpourri will smell like a rubbish dump. So start simply.

- *Package them.* Make little sachets of charged herbs to carry around with you or give them as a spell for someone else. Best to use dried herbs for this so they don't go moldy. I love this method because you can combine herbs and other things to create a powerful mix. And once they've woven their magic, they can be buried or burned.

- *Strew them.* In the Middle Ages, when places and people didn't smell particularly pleasant, herbs and flowers were strewn through rooms so that their fragrance was released when people walked on them. Thanks to our modern-day bathing and cleaning (thank goodness), this is not something that is done often nowadays. But you can create a magical strew to imbue your home with the energies of the plants. Just remember to sweep up well afterward!

- *Remember wild herbs.* The hedgerow is full of beautiful magical herbs you can use—plants that people mainly look on as weeds. How dare they! Get hold of a good book on wild plants—one with clear photographs, if possible—and explore what's on your own doorstep. Your larder of useable magical herbs will really expand and you'll get to know what grows around you.

Herby Falafel Balls (makes 12)

Ingredients for the falafel

480 g./17 oz. canned chickpeas, drained

1 lemon, juiced

1 handful fresh mint

1 handful fresh coriander or parsley

2 spring onions

1 tbsp. plain/all-purpose flour

2 tbsp. vegetable oil

Method for the falafel

1. Chop the spring onions, mint, and coriander or parsley.

2. Put chickpeas, spring onions, lemon juice, and chopped herbs into a blender and blitz until almost smooth, but with a little texture. You can also do this in a bowl with a potato masher.

3. Roll the mixture into 12 small balls, dusting with a little flour if the mixture is sticky.

4. Roll the balls in flour until they are coated.

5. Heat the oil in a frying pan over a medium heat. Add the balls a few at a time, and fry gently for approx. 5 minutes, or until golden.

6. Serve with the herby dip, a few fresh salad leaves, and warm pita bread.

Ingredients for the dip

100 ml./3.5 oz. plain yogurt

1 handful parsley and coriander, finely chopped

1 clove of garlic crushed (optional)

Salt and pepper

Method for the dip

Blend all the ingredients together in a bowl and set aside to infuse.

This is the perfect recipe for sharing all your lovely herbs with others and it's really affordable too. Once you've made these, you will make them again and again. Experiment with whatever herbs take your fancy. You can add chili to give them a kick. To turn these into a substantial meal, add the balls to a simple tomato sauce and serve with steamed rice. Delicious!

Grow Confident in Your Magic

Whether we are just starting out on our magical paths or have been traveling along them for many, many moons, we can all do with a little more confidence, can't we? I really believe that I am on a lifelong journey and won't ever know all things about everything. And to me, that is a wonderful thing! The world is full of mysteries and meanings, with as many interpretations as there are people. No two people are the same and no two beliefs are the same either. So you need to grow confident in what you are doing.

There are so many access points to knowledge these days that information isn't necessarily hard to find. The question is: Does the information you find work for you? I could rattle on about the properties of rosemary, but do you feel that what I am saying resonates with you? No? Then what does? Just because you have an opinion or feeling that isn't in line with what someone else says doesn't make you wrong. It all comes down to having confidence in yourself—and I know that that is sometimes easier said than done. So how do you find that elusive confidence to apply to your magic?

Magic is such a personal practice that there is no one thing that can give you confidence. But here are some ideas that you may find useful:

- *Harm none.* Remember the rule "Harm none" and you won't go far wrong. Keep love at the heart of all you do magically, and you can be sure that you are heading in the right direction. If you keep to these two rules, what's the worst that can happen? Don't let fear stop you from living magically.

- *Learn something every day.* Become an expert in something that speaks to you. Are you interested in herbs? Candles? Colors? Tarot? Learn about them. Knowledge is empowering, and as your knowledge grows, so will your confidence. Check and double-check the accuracy of all your information, but remember to check how it feels for you as well. You can't have confidence in your magic if you don't feel what will work for you. Build on any knowledge you already have so you can understand exactly what you are working with.

- *Make and record plans.* Think about what you want to achieve in a spell or magical working. Cover all the bases you can think of. Do they all safely fall under the "Harm none" guideline? Planning ahead is a great way to gain confidence, but it also helps to write your plan down so you can look back on your magic and see what worked for you and what didn't.

- *Create a magical space.* Set aside a place where you feel comfortable working your spells through before you actually do them. Light a candle or incense to denote that this is a magical time and space for you to work in.

- *Stay positive.* You won't always get things right. Nobody does! We are all human and all make mistakes. Learn from them and move on. Dwelling on mistakes will only get you down and bring in negativity—and none of us needs any more of that in this world. Stay positive and have fun with your magic. Each time you create a spell, you create something unique, because the most important element in magic is you! Remember to compare yourself to *you* and not to others. Other people are not the same as you, so you can never be compared to them.

- *If in doubt, shout!* Try a simple meditation in a wood or a meadow that you see in your mind and call for guidance. Pay attention to what you are shown. There is always help at hand if you need it—in the outside world, via books, or on the Internet. Sadly, not so much by word of mouth anymore, but there is always that inner voice screaming to be heard. So trust your gut reaction and instincts. You know more than you think you do; listen to yourself.

- *Be gentle with yourself.* The fact that you are creating magic under the rule of "Harm none" means you have good intentions at heart. You are an awesome being and should always treat yourself with the love you give out to others. Give yourself time to grow on your path and don't do what we all tend to do at times—beat yourself up. Be kind to yourself and that kindness will shine through in your magic.

WITCHY WAYS TO CELEBRATE MAY

- Decorate your home and altar with combinations of flowers and colors to celebrate the union between the Goddess and the God.

- Work with herbs in your magic by creating spell bags and sachets. Cook with herbs whenever you can.

- Create a spell for strength and wellness by lighting a Beltane candle and burning your spell written on some pretty paper.

- Create a harmonious magical garden with symbols and signs of the craft. Paint pebbles and draw shapes in the earth.

- Get outside and find one useable foraged ingredient for your recipes. This is also good for expanding your plant knowledge.

- Connect with the God aspect by connecting with nearby trees. Spend time touching the tree and water the roots as an offering.

- Make daisy chains as offerings for the Fae folk.

May Folklore

"A swarm of bees in May is worth a load of hay."

"Mist in May, heat in June, makes harvest come right soon."

"If you wash a blanket in May, you will wash one of the family away."

"Those who bathe in May will soon be laid in clay!"

Chapter Four

—◆—

JUNE

The sun is high in the clear blue sky,
It's time to watch the birds fly by.
They dip and dive in the warm summer air,
It's time for a party or a Midsummer fair!

Foods at Their Best in June

Fruit and Vegetables

aubergines, artichokes, asparagus, apricots, broad beans, beetroot, blueberries, black currants, broccoli, courgettes, cherries, carrots, chicory, cucumbers, fennel, french beans, green beans, gooseberries, mange tout, nectarines, new potatoes, onions, peas, red currants, rocket, radishes, runner beans, rhubarb, romaine lettuce, raspberries, sorrel, spinach, spring onions, strawberries, turnips, tomatoes, watercress

Seafood

cod, crab, coley, cockles, Dover sole, gray mullet, haddock, halibut, herring, John Dory, langoustines, lemon sole, lobster, mackerel, pollack, plaice, salmon, sardines, sea trout

Wild Foods

dandelion, daisy, elderflower, fairy ring champignon, lime flowers, marsh samphire, meadowsweet, nasturtium, nettle, plantain, sorrel, sea purslane, sea beet, wild mint, wild rose flower, wild strawberry, wood pigeon

June Correspondences

- *Festival*: Summer solstice (Litha). Symbols include the sun, fire, sunflowers, vegetables, and oak leaves.

- *Moon name*: Strawberry Moon, because it's the height of the strawberry-picking season. Other names include Planting Moon and Green Corn Moon.

- *Astrological signs*: Gemini, May 21–June 20; Cancer, June 21–July 20.

- *Birthstones*: Pearl and moonstone.

- *Nature spirits*: Fire spirits and water nymphs.

- *Animals*: Bees, butterflies, and squirrels.

- *Birds*: Goldfinch and house martin.

- *Trees*: Oak.

- *Flowers*: Dog roses, ox-eyed daisies, wild orchid.

- *Herbs*: Yarrow, fennel, and St. John's wort.

- *Scents*: Honeysuckle, rose, and lavender.

- *Colors*: Red, orange, gold, and yellow.

- *Goddess*: Cerridwin.

- *Powers*: Strength and energy from the sun; blossoming confidence and beauty; dedication.

- *Other*: The Queen's birthday trooping of the colors, the longest day, Environment Day, and the beginning of exams.

Ah, if there's anything more beautiful than a sunny June day in an English garden, I have yet to find it! In theory, June enters bright and warm, with gentle breezes carrying the scent of honeysuckle and roses, jasmine and lilies across the garden and in through your windows. Bliss! That is, if it doesn't roll in with driving rain and howling winds, as it seems to have done over the last few years. No, let's not go there. Let's concentrate on the bright and warm bit, shall we?

June is the time of year when you can't seem to stop your feet from moving you outside to enjoy all things natural. The plants seem alive with the buzzing of honeybees, and the sun is high. This is the month when we celebrate Midsummer, which does seem strange when you look at the calendar. The summer holidays are still over a month away. But look around you in the gardens and hedgerows and you will see nature's own clock at work. Everything is at its best during June, and nature doesn't lie! Life is practically bursting at the seams. Blooms of every description are full and fragrant; fruit is either flowering or ripening with each day that passes; and you are suddenly stricken with that terrible fear of baring flesh! It's so warm that you can't help but don your skimpy tops—or even, oh my goodness, the bathing suit! I do not have a bikini body—never have—and the thought of those pasty white legs being on show sends shudders up my spine. Nope, the best I can manage is a pair of cut-off jeans and a T-shirt. If you're braver than I am, I salute you!

June is all about the sun, and with the longest day occurring in this month, it is a time when you can make the most of the long, lazy evenings. The increase in daylight encourages you to get out there and be part of the magic. It stands to reason that, as a Hedgewitch, I spend lots of time out in the hedgerows—not only gathering their bounty, but just being part of their cycle. The birds are looking after their young, with no time to sit and sing much (we know how that feels). So the hedgerow at this time of the year can be quite silent—barring the hum of the insects, of course. It is a wonderful time to connect with the trees and flowers that line the fields. Close your eyes and feel yourself a part of what is around you. If that field of scarlet poppies is awe-inspiring, it is a time to celebrate the fact that you are part of it!

Look to the trees and you will find that the oak is in flower now. The oak king is said to be locked in a battle with the holly king over each half of the year. June is the time when the oak king is at his strongest, just before the holly king takes over at Midsummer with the drawing in of the nights.

Summer Solstice (Litha)

In June, all focus is on that big round ball in the sky—the sun. Our ancestors tracked their year not by that cute kitten calendar of which we all have variations, but by the movements of the planets, sun, and moon. They knew that Midsummer—June 21, or Litha, as it's also called—was the longest day and shortest night of the year. They knew that this was the time of maximum daylight for doing anything that needed doing outside. So Midsummer was a time of great thanksgiving and celebration. We only have to look at the monuments built to mark the sun's passage at both Midsummer and Midwinter to know how important it was to our ancestors to recognize these times of year.

I am so very blessed to live in Wiltshire, a county of so many ancient monuments. I grew up knowing all about the turning of the Wheel and the celebrations at sun monuments. Every year when I was a child, the police presence around Stonehenge and Avebury Henge grew as the number of people wishing to celebrate the sun increased. It makes me happy to know that so many want to celebrate at these ancient stone circles that were built in line with the sun's path so its rays could shine between the stones as it rose at dawn. Stonehenge is around 5,000 years old and represents such a massive project that it must have been at the heart of ancient British celebrations. In fact, I believe it is the ultimate sun temple. The northeast entrance is perfectly aligned to the Midsummer rising sun and the Midwinter sunset. This can't be a happy accident, and there must have been some very clever builders afoot in Wiltshire!

Avebury Henge is often overlooked in the profusion of monuments in Wiltshire, but it is a place very close to my heart. Not surprising, really, since it's where I live as well! The Henge is part of a complex of ancient features in the Wiltshire landscape—West Kennett Longbarrow, Silbury Hill, the Sanctuary, Hackpen Hill, Piggledean, and Swallowhead Springs are all clustered in this area. These monuments are all amazingly beautiful and were important to our ancestors. At Midsummer, the stone circle comes alive with the beating of drums and people partying till dawn to welcome the rising sun. These features are all so much more accessible here than they are elsewhere. You can get up-close and personal with the stones, walk among them, and really feel the history and energy of this amazing site.

There are many stone monuments littered across the U.K., but every country seems to have its own temples to the sun—Machu Picchu in Peru, the

Dakshinaarka temple at Gaya in India, and the solar temples of Userkaf and Nyuserre in Egypt, just to name a few. The sun has always been worshipped and celebrated across the world. So when we join in the party to honor the sun, we are all walking in the footsteps of our ancestors. How cool is that!

Did our ancestors celebrate Litha, the longest day of the year? In fact, the word "solstice" comes from the Latin word *solstitium*, which means "sun stands still." And that's exactly what the sun seems to do at Litha! The battle between light and dark is an old one. The solstice is a time to celebrate the light, but also to honor the return of the dark as the nights start getting longer. In traditional fire festivals, hilltop fires were lit in honor of the sun to recognize the space between the heavens and the earth. But the solstice is also a time of balance in the year, and because the balance of fire is water, wells and springs were visited at this time as well. People dropped in coins for good luck or bathed in the waters. In Europe, balls of straw were set alight and rolled downhill into a body of water to represent the balance between the elements. Now, I am not for one minute suggesting we all go and set fire to balls of straw and roll them down a hill, nor do I think that many of us are up to bathing in a cold stream at dawn! So what can *we* do to celebrate Litha?

Get outside! Drag the children, your other half, or your pets out into the fresh air and away from the TV. Hit the paddling pool; splash around in the water under the warm sun (always remembering the sunscreen). Stay up late to say goodnight to the sun and tell lots of stories waiting for it to rise again after the shortest night—if you can keep going that long. Light candles in honor of fire and bathe in a flower-scented bath to honor water.

Midsummer's Eve is a magical night when herbs and flowers possess potent healing properties. The veil between our world and the world of the Fae is at its thinnest at this time, so leave offerings of honey and fruit for our fairy friends. Listen for their music as they sing and dance at this special time. And watch out for practical jokes—the Fae love to make mischief!

Sun Spell

A simple sun spell can help you capture the power of this most important time in the sun's journey across our skies. And who doesn't need a bit of that potent energy in their everyday lives? This simple sun spell harnesses the energy of the sun into an amulet (token) that you can carry with you. Call on it whenever you need a bit of that brightness.

You will need:

- A candle and something to light it with—I like to use a red candle because the sun is a fire element, but use any color you have or that speaks to you

- A pinch of dried spice—dried chili flakes, cayenne pepper, or black pepper

- A daisy (ruled by the element of fire)

- A plate or saucer to work from

Gather your spell materials together and go outside into the sunshine. Sit somewhere green and quiet if you can, and hold your candle, spices, and daisy in one hand. Cup your other hand over the top. Concentrate on focusing your energy into what you are holding. Focus on the creation of something that will bring you brightness when you need it.

When you're ready, light the candle carefully and drop wax onto the plate or saucer to create a pool of wax. Extinguish the candle and, working swiftly, sprinkle the spice onto the molten wax. Place the daisy onto the wax and spice. Carefully mould the still-warm wax into a ball or penny shape, enclosing the spices and daisy within it. You can always drip more wax onto the top to ensure that the spell is fully enclosed.

When the wax has cooled, hold the amulet in one hand and raise your hand to the sun. Close your eyes and imagine the brightness and warmth of the sun's energy forming a sphere around your amulet, empowering it with its energy. Say some simple words like:

Power of the sun, charge this spell till it is done.

When you feel that your amulet has absorbed the sun's power, thank the sun for lending you its strength. When you return home, relight your candle and burn it in thanks for the success of your spell.

Carry this amulet with you and reach for it whenever you need to lend the sun's power to whatever you are doing. Use it when a spell needs an extra boost, or on a cold gray day that leaves you feeling down, or when a friend is in need of some brightness at a difficult time. This powerful little spell can also be recharged by holding the amulet up to the sun whenever you need a boost. You can use it as a focus in fire spells as well.

After all this talk about fire, I think it's time to head off to the kitchen to make something to balance out that fire. Creamy pudding comes to mind.

Solstice Strawberry Pudding (serves 6)

Ingredients for the strawberry layer

200 g./7 oz. strawberries, wild if you can find them,
   otherwise normal strawberries are fine

2 handsful of rose petals or 2 tbsp. of rosewater

2 tbsp. icing sugar

A large sprig of mint

Ingredients for the rice pudding

1 vanilla pod or 1 tsp. vanilla extract

125 g./4.5 oz. pudding rice

800 ml./27 oz. Jersey or whole milk

250 ml./8.5 oz. double cream

50 g./2 oz. caster sugar

Method

1. If you are using ordinary strawberries, slice any large ones in half and keep any smaller ones whole. For wild strawberries, gently rinse and drain.

2. Place the strawberries into a bowl with the rose petals or rosewater, the icing sugar, and the sprig of mint torn into several pieces. Let stand for around a half hour for the flavors to combine.

3. In a pan, mix the rice, cream, milk, and sugar together. Split the vanilla pod and scrape out the seeds. Add the seeds to the pan, along with the pod. If using vanilla extract, add this to the mix in the pan.

4. Place the pan on the heat and bring to a simmer. Stir gently for approx. 30 minutes, until the rice is soft and tender and has absorbed most of the liquid. The pudding should be fairly liquid in texture, but it will thicken as it cools. Add a little more milk if it starts to look too thick before the rice is sufficiently cooked.

5. Remove the mint from the strawberry mixture and stir to combine the flavors.

6. Serve in a glass layering the strawberries and rice pudding to make a pretty parfait. Garnish with a few wild strawberries, rose petals, and a mint leaf.

This pudding is at its best when the rice is still warm. but it is also delicious cold. So any leftovers can be kept till the next day. Experiment with whatever soft fruit you have on hand—raspberries, blueberries, and apricots all work really well.

STRESS TIME

So far, all the talk about June has been about the solstice—which is understandably important. But I bet many of you are dealing with something this month that is a little harder to handle and certainly is never celebrated—exam time! Oh yes, it's here again—those stress-filled days of over-anxious children who either cram till their heads look as if they may explode, or go the other way and try to pretend it really isn't happening! I think I had one of each of these types and handling either one at this time is not easy—ever! You will never understand what it's like according to the little darlings. You have *never* had it as hard as they have. In a way, it is kind of true. Examinations at school seem to have become more important than ever, and the pressure on kids seems to increase every year. But we have all been through it, and I certainly remember it was not a fun time when I was young.

The tantrums, though. That's something I never had the luxury of throwing. I would never have dared with my mum. But these days, children seem to be more forthcoming with their feelings—and how! Daughter number two was probably the worst at exam time. The complete panic-fear of failure struck and manifested itself in tears, rows, and an overly meticulous preparation that required the color coding of every piece of review material—to the point that the coding took up more time than the actual review! It's not just the kids, though. Whether you're back in school, taking a driving test, or just after more credentials at work, exams and the stress they cause can be really hard to control. Time for a little magical help, methinks!

Magical Stress-Busters

The best way to beat stress is to find out the root cause of the problem and tackle it. In most cases, that cures the feeling straight away! But sometimes, when there's just no getting away from the fact that you are frazzled and you can't change the cause or understand the reasons for the stress, reaching for something magical can be a good option. Here are some methods I find helpful for dealing with stress:

- *Breathe.* Sounds simple, because we all do it without thinking, but it does really work to focus on your breathing. Remember, your breath is a magical part of you and the air you breathe is a magical part of the world around you. Go and find a tree and exchange your breath with it. Trees breathe in carbon dioxide, which is what you breathe out. And they breathe out oxygen, which is what you breathe in. How handy is that! This magical exchange can work as an energy exchange. So ask the tree to take your stress in return for some of its strength. This is a really effective method of stress-busting. But always remember to leave an offering for the tree—maybe some water to pour around its roots.

- *Meditate.* Go on a journey in your mind to a magical place. It is nice to have a safe place to visit without having actually to leave your home. Create a grove of tranquility in your mind's eye that you can visit anytime you need some peace.

Meditating can take some practice, however. I have to admit that it doesn't come easily to me. But remember that meditation is just picturing something in your mind; if you can see it there, then it is real. Spend time creating your magical mental space, and place a box in there that you can pour your stress into. It really does work, and it really is magical.

- *Herbs.* There are some tried-and-tested herbs that have been proven to reduce stress levels and induce a feeling of peace. Chamomile tea is a wonderful natural calmer and lavender naturally induces a feeling of calm and peace. Red clover, tarragon, rosemary, dill, St. John's wort, and sage all work well to calm and soothe you. Burn essential oil or make a stress sachet with one or more of these herbs. Turn to it when you need a bit of a hand.

- *Candles.* Burn that stress away with candle magic. Simply write the word "stress" with a pin along the side of a candle and light it. Watch it as it burns away your word and your stress. Feel it melt away.

- *Shout it out.* Get outside into the hedgerow, park, or garden, and shout out your stress. Yes, you may look slightly nutty, but this really can help to relieve that built-up adrenaline. When you do this, you release your stress for Mother Nature to recycle into "good vibrations." Remember, all released negativity gets recycled into something more positive, and the best way to shake loose from the grip of stress is simply to let it go!

Now, amid all the stress and upheaval that may rear its head at exam time, there is another event that seems to have snuck in under the radar in the U.K.—the prom. I know that, in America, this is something that you are used to and are probably well prepared for. But in the U.K., it is a relatively new phenomenon and certainly not something I was prepared for at all. It's like organizing a mini-wedding—with hairdos, nails, makeup, cars, corsages, dates, and the all-important dress to find and pay for. How did this happen? The most glamorous thing I ever went to was a school dance—and I paid for it myself!

Daughter number one's prom was a time filled with cold sweats about money and transport. The day of the prom, her hair wasn't right (a few tantrums) and the dress didn't fit (a few tears). Finally, I waved her off with her friends looking absolutely gorgeous in a stretch Hummer. Then I received a phone call after about an hour asking me to come pick her up because she was bored! Daughter number two was even worse, because she has a tendency to overplan everything. So the dress took many fittings, the hair had to be perfect, and the cost of the jewelry alone was more than I spent on my entire wedding. She wafted off to the prom in a stretch limo with her friends and, thankfully, stayed for the entire event. But I was a bundle of nerves and close to a breakdown after the whole experience!

Stress is a strange thing. You never know when it will strike, or what will tip you over the edge. And you just have to ride it out like a rollercoaster. I tend to cope in the best way I know how—with a little magic, either hitting the kitchen or hitting my head against a brick wall!

Connecting with the Outside World

Working as a solitary Hedgewitch is an extremely rewarding path. You work as a single energy with the world around you, quietly making each day magical for you and those around you, for the greater good of all. But sometimes, it can be a lonely path, with no one to talk to about your magic or beliefs, no one to connect with or even to exchange ideas with. On the other hand, a coven or group may not necessarily be the way you want to go. Because we are all human, groups have a tendency to get a bit cliquey. You know what I mean—he said/she said stuff. Groups that manage to maintain a balance are rare, but they do exist. So if you are after a group setting for your rituals and magic and you find a good one, hold on tight to it!

In general, however, we Hedgewitches like to work alone. So how do we connect with others to share all our magical stuff? Well, if you have a local shop where you get your witchy supplies, chances are others like you will frequent the same shop—so get chatting with them. If someone notices your pentacle necklace and asks a question—chat! Welcome interest in what you believe and practice, and have confidence in your own path. I know, however, that not everyone is as fortunate as I am to live somewhere where alternative beliefs are accepted. If this is the case for you and you want to meet like-minded people, you may need to travel farther afield to a witchy fair or a solstice celebration. People with the same ideals tend to gather together to honor the festivals, so head to your nearest monument or hilltop. If you're there, chances are others will be too.

By far the most popular way to connect with others is now online. We are so fortunate to have the Internet, and we should all make use of this modern technology if we can. The online world opens the doors to a world of Hedgewitchery that our ancestors could only dream of! Facebook and social networking sites can provide links to others with interests similar to yours. They are meeting places for like-minded folks to chat and interact. I have met so many wonderful people through my site—they are my online family! There are so many ideas that have now been put online by people sharing with others that the Internet should be celebrated and not feared.

Of course, you should never place yourself in harm's way. Always follow safe online practices. Research and check any groups or communities that interest you and remember, you don't have to give out any information you don't want to. Online, you can exchange ideas and thoughts, get involved in celebrations and forums, and feel a part of something. You may still be working alone, but there is a wealth of knowledge there at your fingertips. There is much to be gained by sharing knowledge in any way we can, and online is a great way to do it—a bit like reading a book and then having a chat about it at a book club.

Remember, it's not just about connecting with other people on your path; it's also about your connection to the world in general. Everything around us has a connection to us all. The elements, plants and animals, the earth, sky, ocean, and fields—all are part of our shared reality. So we need to reinforce our connection to them every single day. Touch base with what is around you; help where you can; heal whenever it is needed; volunteer if you have the time; make a difference. Make a mark on the world. Become at one with everything and everyone. Seeing all aspects of the world and acknowledging your connection to other things and other people will strengthen your magic.

Simple Connection Ritual

This ritual is a good way to put out a call to like-minded people to come into your life. It is one you can do daily, until you reach your goal. For the ritual, you will need wool or embroidery thread in three colors—one that you feel represents you, one to represent your path, and one to represent others. I have found that charity shops and yard sales are great places to pick up affordable balls of wool or thread.

Sit somewhere comfortable and take a long length of each of your colored threads so you have three strands. With them laid out in front of you, knot the strands together at the top and start to braid them together carefully. (I have found this is easier if you work at a table away from helpful cats' paws!) Do each braid slowly and deliberately, from right to center and then from left to center. As you braid, say some simple words over and over as a chant, something like:

Connections for me, so mote it be!

Braid the strands together a little every day for nine days. At the end of the nine days, knot the two ends together to form a circle. Place the circle of braided thread on a safe surface and light a tea light in the center. Say:

The circle's complete, new friends I will meet!

Allow the candle to burn down safely if you can. Once your spell's complete, bury your circle of thread, returning your spell to the earth for recycling. Your energy and call have been sent. Look out for new opportunities and situations that present themselves to you, and be active in following leads to connections. Remember, magic will only work if you are the driving force behind it!

Reaping Summer's Bounty

With all this time spent outside and with the garden at its height, all the beautiful blooms around you are practically screaming to be picked. It's hard not to gather them all and plonk them in a vase. They can brighten up any room in your home and make a gorgeous gift for a friend when you pop round for coffee. But there is so much more you can do with your flowers than just display them. Here are some ideas that you can use at home with your beautiful blooms:

- *Eat them.* Now, I do not suggest that you go around munching on any old flower. But some are edible and delicious. Get a good book on edible blooms and have a go at introducing one or two of them into your cooking. Some of my favorites are rose petals, herbs like chives and thyme, violets, pansies, marigolds, borage, chamomile, and (my all time favorite) lavender.

- *Drink them.* Add them to drinks or ice cubes before freezing, or try them in cakes and salads.

- *Dry them.* Hang small bunches of flowers in a warm, dark place, making sure the stems are secured so they don't fall as they shrink and dry. You can use these dried flowers to make all sorts of things, from a simple arrangement to a pretty decoration or picture. This is a wonderful way to preserve a special bouquet.

- *Bathe in them.* Add a couple of handsful to your bath to bathe in the essences of the plant. You will feel like a princess or prince, and the water will be infused with the properties of the flower you choose. If you don't fancy scooping out loose petals, tie them loosely in a muslin square and drop this into your bath instead.

- *Press them.* Place small blooms carefully in a flower press or under heavy books between tissue paper, and leave them to press for a couple of weeks. Use them to decorate lampshades or picture frames, or place them in your Book of Shadows.

- *Strew them.* Mix together a few beautiful petals and strew them around your home. They will impart a delicate fragrance and magically charge the air with their properties. I like to use rose petals and lavender in the bedroom for romance and peace.

- *Repel pests.* Some flowers repel flies, mosquitoes, and rodents, so they are well worth using in the home. Hang bunches of lavender, basil, marigolds, or mint over your door to help prevent flies, and sprinkle dried lavender flowers at access points for mice to repel them.

- *Bask in them.* Simmer a couple of handsful of rose petals in pure water, strain, and use as a tonic for your skin after cleansing to ease redness and skin irritations. Always do a patch test first.

- *Speak their language.* Most flowers have a language attached to them—red roses are for love, lavender for peace, dandelions for happiness, etc. Learn about a new flower every time one comes into your life. Then start to send messages to your loved ones with them.

- *Spell with them.* Include flowers in your spells or sachets to add a soft energy to your magic and bring their properties to aid your goal. Place them on your altar as an offering.

- *Cure with them.* So many flowers have medicinal uses, from St. John's wort for depression to chamomile for stress. Research how flowers can help you with some simple remedies at home, or use flower essences already infused with the flower's energy.

Rose Petal Jam
(makes 4-6 220 ml./6.5 oz. jars)

Jams and jellies made with flowers can bring a whole new flavor to your table. Here's a recipe for fragrant rose petal jam. You can also try it with dandelion or red clover for a different taste of the garden. Always remember to use flowers that are free from sprays and pesticides, and watch out for our little bug friends that may be lurking in the petals!

Ingredients

340 g./12 oz. rose petals—the deeper the color,

the darker the jam

1 lb. jam sugar, with added pectin

2 pints water

2 lemons, juiced

Method

1. Trim the white pith from the base of the each of the flower petals and rinse. This takes a while, but smells lovely. Have a glass of something to help pass the time!

2. Gently heat the water and the lemon juice in a saucepan.

3. Stir in the sugar, and heat until the sugar has dissolved; don't boil.

4. Add half of the rose petals and simmer gently for around 5 minutes.

5. Bring the mixture to a boil, add the rest of the petals, and boil the jam for another 5 minutes.

6. Test to see if it's ready by spooning a teaspoon of the jam onto a cold plate. If the jam wrinkles when you push it gently with your finger, it's ready. If not, give it another minute or so.

7. Pour into warm sterilized jars and seal tightly.

This jam is a wonderful taste of summer to spread on your scones and bread, or to use as a topping for a light summer cheesecake. One of my favorite ways to use it is simply to stir it through thick Greek yogurt. If you've never tried rose petal jam before, you're in for a treat. I bet you'll make it every year.

Witchy Ways to Celebrate June

- Decorate your home and altar with fragrant blooms, and light candles to represent the sun.

- Connect with the fairies by leaving an offering of milk, honey, or sweet bread under a bramble bush. Sit in the quiet of sunrise and sunset to see the Fae folk.

- Spell for purification by creating a Midsummer fire and making a protective talisman of summer herbs. Cast illness aside by throwing a pouch of herbs into the cleansing flames.

- Come together with others, either in person or online, to celebrate the longest day. Make a connection.

- Get out and about, and find both an oak and a holly tree. Bow in respect to both at this time of their yearly battle.

June Folklore

"A calm June puts the farmer in tune."

"June damp and warm does the farmer no harm."

"Summer doesn't start till the elder is in flower."

Chapter Five

———◆———

JULY

It's time to rest and picnic in the fields,
It will be soon time for the cutting of the yields.
But for a while, rest your head and sleep in the sun,
For this is a month to find laughter and fun!

Foods at Their Best in July

Fruits and Vegetables

artichokes, aubergines, apricots, broccoli, beetroot, blueberries, black currants, broad beans, cherries, courgettes, cucumbers, coley, fennel, greengages, gooseberries, garlic, green beans, kohlrabi, loganberries, mulberries, nectarines, onions, peaches, potatoes, peas, plums, raspberries, rocket, runner beans, red currants, radishes, raspberries, salad leaves, sorrel, spinach, strawberries, Swiss chard, tomatoes, watercress

Seafood

cod, crab, clams, cockles, Dover sole, gray mullet, haddock, halibut, herring, John Dory, lobster, langoustines, lemon sole, monkfish, mackerel, plaice, squid, sea bream, scallops, sea bass, sardines, salmon, whelks

Wild Foods

crab apples, cep, chanterelles, English lamb, fairy ring champignon, giant puffball, gorse flower, green walnuts, marsh samphire, rabbit, sea purslane, wild blackberries, wild mint, wild rose flower, wild strawberry, wood pigeon

July Correspondences

- *Festival:* None this month.

- *Moon name:* Buck Moon, because the buck deer start growing velvety hair-covered antlers this month. Other names include Summer Moon, Hay Moon, and Thunder Moon.

- *Astrological signs:* Cancer, June 21–July 20; Leo, July 21–August 20.

- *Birthstones:* Ruby and carnelian.

- *Nature spirits:* Earth-based Fae and goblins.

- *Animals:* Deer, mice, and all sea creatures.

- *Birds:* Buzzards and birds of prey.

- *Trees:* Elm.

- *Flowers:* Jasmine, honeysuckle, travelers' joy, crane's bill, meadowsweet.

- *Herbs:* Lavender, feverfew, mint, and marjoram.

- *Scents:* Honeysuckle, rose, and jasmine.

- *Colors:* Deep violet and green.

- *Goddess:* Branwen.

- *Powers:* Energy of the sun and earth; grounding and abundance.

- *Other:* Start of the crop circle season and the school holidays. St. Swithin's Day.

Ah July! The hot and hazy days of the summer are here at last—we hope. The hedgerow is speckled with beautiful wildflowers and the crops stand golden in the fields. You spend your evenings taking long country walks in the cooling time of the day, and picnic in the fields at the weekend, right? Well, that's the dream. But in reality, it's either raining or so hot that you spend your time walking round in as few clothes as possible, punctuating the still air with the words: "I like it hot, but there's hot and there's hot!" Certainly in Britain, we are never happy with the weather—too hot, too cold, too wet. We rarely find it just right!

Weather aside, as we go hurtling through the year (I swear time is speeding up), this is the month when we start to think about vacations. Funny how we head off to sunny climates at the height of the best weather. Are you a hop-on-a-plane-to-a-beach kind of person, or a have-to-fill-every-moment-with-activity kind of person? I am definitely a beach girl—piña colada in hand on a lounge chair, normally in the shade in an I-like-it-hot-but-it's-too-hot-here kind of way. I have never felt the urge to jump off cliffs with just a rope for company, however. Nor do I feel the need to water ski, surf, or involve myself in anything more athletic than a doggie paddle around a pool or a paddle in the sea!

I do, however, love going away on holiday if I get the chance. And I feel it is a real blessing to be able to immerse yourself in another country's culture. How lucky we are to be able to reach all across the world in hours, when our ancestors took days, or even months, to make a pilgrimage just across their own land. Travel by plane, train, boat, and car has made it possible for us to reach all the places our hearts desire—barring financial issues, of course. And the fact is that it's not cheap to travel anywhere these days, so we are more often than not limited by cost as much as time.

HOLIDAYS ABROAD

If you are lucky enough to make it across the seas and discover a new land, make it an opportunity to learn about the magical practices of the land you are visiting. Every country has a past, and the ancestors of that place will have left clues to the practices of old. Seek them out! Learn all you can about where you're heading before you travel, and actually get off the lounge chair for a moment and speak to the locals. Many cultural beliefs are represented by monuments and landscapes, so try to visit something of significance at least once before returning to your lounge chair to top up your tan (and your alcohol levels). We may be witches, but we all need a little rest and recuperation sometimes!

And don't leave your magic at home when you travel. Remember, magic is within you. So see each holiday not only as a rest, but also as an ideal chance to create some new magic—something that you wouldn't ordinarily be able to do at home. The beach gives you an amazing chance to work water magic with the sea. The local flora and fauna will have different energies than what you left at home. The food will hold a different energy as well. Whether you are near mountains, streams, deserts, snow, jungles, or forests, take some time to connect with the new landscape that will be your home for a week or two. Make your mark magically; cast a spell for the country you are visiting—for its people and its environment. Send blessings and thanks for the chance to be where you are, even for a short time. Write your spell in the sand or snow, or spell it out with shells or pebbles. Or symbolically water a dry plant, asking that all plants may be nourished too. Make a difference by picking up litter if you see it; find a feather to use in a spell to bless all animal life. And smile—magically doing these things nourishes your soul as well as makes a difference.

Tired now—back to the sun lounger, or maybe it's time for dinner? I never seem to stop eating while I'm away and I think it is a given that most of us put on a bit of weight while we're traveling. The food of other countries is fascinating. I really believe you can feel the past through a dish, how it has evolved down the generations and what crops the country produces and lives on. It's funny that, when on holiday, we eat things that we wouldn't even dream of buying and cooking at home.

I love to bring a little of the food culture of where I visit back to my kitchen when I return home, and really enjoy experimenting with new spices and herbs to try and recreate dishes from holidays—not always successfully I might add! But here's one I came up with after my last holiday to Tunisia that I hope you'll enjoy. Whenever I make it, I always focus on blessing the country and asking for prosperity and peace for its people.

Happy Hot Harissa Kebabs (serves 4)

Ingredients for harissa paste

12 dried red chili peppers

3 cloves garlic

1/2 tsp. salt

2 tbsp. olive oil

1 tsp. coriander seeds

1 tsp. ground caraway seeds

1/2 tsp. cumin seeds

Method for harissa paste

1. Soak the dried chilies in boiling water for approx. 30 minutes to soften.

2. Drain the chilies and remove any stems and seeds if you don't like it too spicy.

3. With a pestle and mortar, pound together the soaked chilies, garlic, salt, and olive oil until they form a paste.

4. Add the remaining spices and pound them into the paste to release their flavors.

5. Store in an airtight container. Drizzle the top of the paste with olive oil to help keep it fresh. This paste will keep for around a month in the fridge.

Ingredients for the kebabs

500 g./17.5 oz. pork fillet, cut into cubes

1 large aubergine, cut into chunks

1 large red onion, cut into pieces

Method for the kebabs

1. Soak some wooden skewers in cold water for 30 minutes. You can do this while soaking your chilies.

2. When soaked, thread alternate pork, aubergine, and red onion pieces onto the skewers.

3. Brush the skewers liberally with the harissa paste.

4. Place the skewers on a hot griddle pan or a barbeque and cook for 7–8 minutes, turning frequently, until the pork is just cooked through and starting to char around the edges.

5. Finish the skewers with a squeeze of fresh lemon juice and serve with a simple salad, couscous, and pita bread. Now, where did I put my passport?

HOLIDAYS AT HOME

Most years, I don't get to go abroad. I imagine it's probably the same for a lot of us. But this is a blessing as well, I think, because it gives us a chance to explore closer to home. We are completely part of the landscape in which we live, whether it be town or countryside. But we very rarely actually explore it. Holidays at home, which don't involve jetting off to other lands, usually mean visiting another part of our own country. This is wonderful, but sometimes I think we should declare a holiday when we actually stay at home. No packing, no airports, no passports, and no need to hear the immortal words that come from all children's mouths at one time or another: "Are we there yet?"

Staying at home for a holiday does mean enforcing some strict rules on yourself, however: no washing, no housework, and no shopping allowed. And no sitting in front of the television watching daytime soaps. Stay-at-home holidays are about getting outside and exploring the magic of where you are. You need strong willpower to do this, and you have to turn a blind eye to any chaos that may ensue in the house. Your hands may be itching to drag out the Hoover or scrub the bathroom; but it is a holiday, so no chores allowed!

Now, it is all very well to say this, but I have to be honest—it's not something I can do. I have a compulsion to wander round with a damp cloth whenever I'm at home, and I can never look at the tumbleweed of fluff blowing across my floor without doing something about it. I can just about manage a day or two, however, so a short holiday at home does work for me—just on a small scale. It's really all about taking some time out for yourself, taking yourself back to that magical place inside you that you don't get the time to visit very often. Here are some ideas for a couple of days at home on holiday.

Magical Maps

Get out into the landscape around you, and connect with whatever is within walking distance. Really look at the trees and plants and any wildlife you see. Take along a small book to help identify plants and a notebook to mark down what you find.

Try drawing a map of the area you live in; but instead of marking down roads and streets, mark where the big oak tree is, where the blackberries can be found, where you can gather your clover, and where the wildlife cuts through the landscape on their travels. Build up your magical map whenever you get the chance to go for a wander. As you grow in your magic, this will become a valuable tool to help find what you need.

Witchy Walks

A witchy walk is different from an everyday walk, because it doesn't have a destination. Most of us always know exactly where we are going when we leave the house, but on a witchy walk you are guided by what is shown to you. I love to do witchy walks; they can be so magical. Before you set off from home, take a few moments to decide roughly how long you want to walk and any questions or decisions you want help with.

When you are ready, exit your front door with focus and look for a sign of which way to go. It may be a bird flying past or the breeze blowing in a certain direction. Follow the way you are shown and look for markers along the way—a feather, a stone, the flow of the river, or a swirling leaf can all be markers on your journey. This is a magical walk, so take your directions from what's around you. Walk with complete focus on what your senses show you—a smell may take you one way, a noise may take you another.

Stop when you have walked for roughly the time you set aside, or until you feel you have obtained what you need. You may be led to a flower or a tree. If so, find out what that flower represents and how it is associated with you. Or you may have been led to a view or landmark. If so, learn about it and try to relate it to your question or problem. Keep your mind open and you will be taken on the right path.

This is something that you should do with a friend or partner, if only to keep you safe. It's never a good idea to go wandering off on your own without knowing where you're going. Your walking partner can be a silent companion, there only to ensure that you know where you are and how to get home. And make sure you take your phone and some food and water with you in case you get lost along the way.

A Day with the Elements

Plan to spend a day with the elements. Take some food and water and set out to find and connect with all the elements—earth, air, fire, and water. Follow your heart; it will tell you where to go. A hilltop is a wonderful place to connect with air; a river, stream, or canal can put you in touch with water; a field of crops can ground you in earth; a sunny warm spot can connect you to fire. If one or more of these elementals aren't accessible where you live, set out for your element day with your own supplies to celebrate the elements—water, a candle, incense, and earth or salt. Find somewhere beautiful to sit—in a park or even in a garden—and create and connect to your own elemental space.

Spend time focusing on each element in turn. Consider what each brings to your life and how you can use it in your magic. When you return home, take time to focus on the fifth element—ether, or space. This is such a vital element that we sometimes overlook it, but we shouldn't. I find that looking into a dark bowl or cauldron is a good way to focus on ether. I see it as the big melting pot in which all elements combine.

FIRE MAGIC

Fire is the element that I believe connects us most strongly to our ancestors. We all use fire in our day-to-day lives to perform pure alchemy. Since the first discovery of the spark, we have built fires and looked into the flames, sent wishes to the heavens in their whirling smoke, and transformed our food magically with their heat. So when we look to the element of fire for our magic, we are tapping into something strong and primal—something ancient and powerful that links us closely to all of those who have gone before us. When we cook, we work magically with the fire element, but sometimes it is wonderful to work with this element in a different way. Sometimes it helps to get back to basics.

Although there are table-top fires available for indoor use—and, of course, there is candle magic—I like to work my fire magic outside. This allows my intent to be carried away. It is so much safer, and it saves all that flapping around under the fire alarm with a tea towel. Come on, you know you've done it too!

When you are ready for fire magic, you must first decide where to build your fire. Unless you have an actual fire pit in your garden, be aware of all the things around your yard that could go up in flames without a little care. Avoid building your fire next to a fence or shed. If you build your fire out in the countryside, always consider the worse-case scenario and make sure you prepare properly. And keep things small. Always have water on hand to extinguish your flames at the end of your ritual.

Next, gather twigs for your fire. Keep the pieces small; you don't need a raging inferno to produce powerful fire magic. Different woods give off different kinds of smoke; but as long as they are dry, any twigs will burn well. Avoid using elder twigs, however, as they don't burn well. And you should never burn elder anyway, as it is considered to be the "witches' tree." Extremely bad luck!

Once you have a safe location for your fire and something to burn, you can get started.

Fire Ritual for Healing

You will need:

A small piece of paper

A pencil or pen

A pinch of dried thyme

Light your fire, keeping it small and contained. As the flames start to catch, focus on them dancing in front of you. Let the flames lull you into a strong focus on your intent. Think of the world being healed from all damage, being restored to health and vibrancy. Keep your intent pure and strong as you watch the flames gather intensity. Raise the power and energy within you in line with the flames.

When you feel full of power and focused on your goal, write your words on the piece of paper. Speak from the heart and keep your words simple and pure. If you are sending healing to someone else, focus on the image of that person being well as you write. If you are sending out healing to the world, focus on Mother Nature being strong and vibrant. Always keep your mind on the desired outcome of your ritual; see things in your mind's eye as you wish them to be.

With focus, place the piece of paper carrying your words carefully into the flames. As the fire engulfs the paper, say a few simple words to add your energy to the outcome—something like:

I now send healing to . . .

Watch as the paper burns and is transformed into smoke that is carried up to the sky, carrying your healing with it. As the flames start to die down, take your pinch of dried thyme and sprinkle it on the glowing twigs. Watch as the thyme is transformed to smoke and is carried away to heal. Say something like:

Thyme heals all wounds; may this thyme heal . . .

Watch as the smoke from your fire now rises, taking your intent with it. Imagine it floating off to touch those to whom you have sent healing, bathing them in golden light.

As you finish your fire ritual, remember to say thank you for the success of your spell. Simply close your eyes and see all the elements coming together to carry your energy where it is needed. See all the ancestors who have gone before lending their energy to the success of your goal. Say something simple, like:

I thank you for your help.

If you can, allow your fire to burn safely away while you focus on the healing being sent where it is needed. Otherwise, extinguish your fire completely and return the area to the way it was before you leave.

This fire ritual is a simple one, but it can be extremely powerful. You can use it for all sorts of workings, not just for healing. Thanks and blessings can be carried away on the smoke. And, because fire also purifies, it can be used to free you or someone else from stress and worries, transforming these negative forces into smoke to be carried away and recycled into positivity. This ritual is also a wonderful way to communicate with the ancestors, the world of spirit, and Mother Nature. Always remember to keep your words simple and your goal focused. It is *your* intent in the spell that gives it power.

COOKING WITH FIRE

How many of us get outside and cook with fire these days? The magical transformation of food through fire seems to be reserved for months like July, when the sun is shining and we drag the cobweb-covered barbecue out of the shed. The air becomes heady with the smell of charcoal and—a little like the common cold—the need to cook over fire spreads like a virus across the nation. You can't help yourself—one sniff of someone else's outdoor cooking and off you race to the nearest shop for some burgers or sausages. One warm sunny day can cause a nationwide shortage of burger buns, resulting in foraging around the shops trying to find an alternative. Many a burger has been cut down to fit in a hotdog bun in my kitchen!

Barbecuing not only transforms the food that's cooked, it transforms any man into the greatest chef that ever lived! Suddenly, the man who can't figure out how to turn on the oven becomes the Master of the Flames—apron strapped on and tongs in hand. He is hunter/gatherer, and capable of feeding a small army—all due to a small pile of charcoal and a hint of sunshine. I say "he," because it does tend to be the man who believes that only he is capable of cooking outdoors. But, of course, many women also appreciate not being tied to the oven and become possessive of the title of Master of the Flames for the day. I suppose it is no wonder that we get so excited at the prospect of cooking over hot coals. It is a subconscious link to our ancestors, a primitive urge that is present in all of us to feed our loved ones.

But cooking over an open fire can be risky business. Food that we ordinarily just pop into the oven now needs careful handling and precise cooking times. And raw meat can have a very nasty after-effect, if you know what I mean. I really believe these dangers can be overcome by cooking outside more often, and actually learning how to use fire to transform food safely. When the skies are gray and there's rain in the air, we all give up on outside cooking. But maybe it's time to be brave and get out there in all kinds of weather—just to get back to basics and work in a different way with our food.

The safest way to experiment with cooking food over a fire is to use vegetables. This eliminates the risk of food poisoning from undercooked meats and gives you lots of choice of flavors. Try making something outdoors at least once a week to get back in touch with the alchemy of fire—that is, if someone indoors doesn't take the tongs hostage!

MAGICAL SPONTANEITY

Magic in our everyday lives doesn't need long-winded planning and the construction of elaborate spells and rituals—although these can be wonderful for festivals, or if you have a lot of time. Living magically every day only requires that you be spontaneous, that you have confidence in what you are doing, and that you work with good intentions in your heart. It's a bit like gourmet meals. They're wonderful to cook every so often, but completely impractical to cook every day!

You don't need to be gliding around in your cloak with your wand in hand to create magic all the time. In fact, some of the best magic you can create comes from using whatever is on hand and doing what you normally do. You are the power behind your spells. So, simply by connecting with something and speaking or thinking a few simple words, you can live magically. Anything—from herbs, to candles, to water, to simply holding something in your hand—can carry your magical intent out into the world.

Now, because your magic is unique to you, it's really tricky suggesting things for you to use or do. Your magic wouldn't be spontaneous then, would it? But hopefully these few ideas will give you some confidence in making your own spontaneous magic:

- *Herbs.* Use herbs for simple spell bags, in your cooking, or for tea.

- *Candles.* Light candles or incense with a few simple words of thanks or blessings.

- *Jewelry.* Empower your jewelery to act as your protection. Simply ask that it protect you with a magical white light as you wear it.

- *Water.* Use water for purification spells for yourself or others. Empower it in the sun or moon's light for healing or cleansing.

- *Wood.* Anything wooden can be used to represent the trees, or you can bring in flowers to represent Mother Nature.

- *Cleaning.* Bless your home as you clean with a wipe of your cloth and a silent "Blessed be."

- *Food.* Stir spells into your food, and give a blessing before you eat.

- *Animals.* Give thanks and blessings for all animals as you stroke and feed your pets.

- *Chants.* Chant for peace for the world as you get into bed each night.

The list of how you can use your magic is endless. Remember not to think of it as a separate practice, however. Your magic should be a part of how you live your life, and how you celebrate it—every day.

Your Book of Shadows

Wherever you are on your magical path, a Book of Shadows can be a very important part of your journey. It is your magical diary of sorts—a place where you can put down all your magical spells and rituals, tips to help you improve, and your musings. As you progress down your path, your book will become a valuable source of information about what you have done and what has worked for you. It is your legacy as well—something that will hold all your knowledge in written form for future generations.

So starting a Book of Shadows is a wonderful thing to do. Here are a few tips to get you started:

- *Choose your book.* A notebook or binder with loose-leaf pages are both great options, because you can move things around to create sections and add pages as you go. Decorate whatever you are going to use with symbols and signs that denote its magical content to you. Pretty wrapping paper makes a great cover that can be changed easily if you fancy something different.

- *Create a belief page.* Make the first page of your book a bit like your mission statement. Write down what you believe. Do you follow the Goddess? Is there a particular one with whom you associate? Do you want to practice with spells? Is there an element with which you feel affiliated? Put down all your core beliefs about your craft and leave space to add to your list. You're bound to grow as you progress.

- *Add correspondence pages.* Write down the phases of the moon and their magical meanings, color and herb charts, and all about the eight festivals of the year.

This will become a great reference for you. Color-coding these entries can help you find information quickly and easily.

- *Record spells and rituals.* Write down any rituals or spells you use or create, whether they worked for you, and whether they need any changes. Write down any magical work you do for others, too. This is a good way to record the success of your magical practices.

- *Keep track of hints and tips.* Make a record of any hints and tips you come across. You never know when they may come in handy!

- *Relate stories and tales.* Write down your dreams, if you can remember them. Include any stories or poems that you hear and like as well. If something inspires you, write it down.

- *Follow the seasons.* Include nature in your book by writing down what is changing through the year. Include pressed flowers and leaves, or drawings.

- *Document recipes.* Record any recipes that you come across and write down any magical associations that may go with them. Include whom you cooked them for and whether they actually worked.

- *Date everything.* Always include a date next to your entries. It can be really useful to look back on this timeline, and it will give you a good idea of how your journey is progressing throughout the year.

Over time, writing in your Book of Shadows will become part of your daily magical practice. Remember, it is all about you. So put your heart and soul into your entries. Record your journey and all the laughter and tears you encounter along the way.

Surviving School Holidays

The joy of mid-July! Sun shining and flip-flops out, not a care in the world as you float around in your magical summer haze. And then—what's that you hear? The ringing of the end-of-term bell and—horror of horrors—school's out and it's summer holiday time. Your hands go clammy and you get that sinking feeling of doom. The next six weeks stretch out in front of you like an endless stretch of beach with no bar! How on this earth are you ever going to survive? Every year it's the same. You are faced with overexposure to those sweet little faces, not only at home, but in the shops, in the woods—just about anywhere you want to be, there they are!

The "summer holiday dread" feeling is something that all parents feel, so I asked my friends who have children—either borrowed or their own—what their strategies are for getting through the long break. If you are the proud parent of one or more little witches or wizards, here's my quick guide on how to survive the *long* summer break:

- *Get them outside.* Come rain or shine, the great outdoors is the biggest classroom in the world. Remember that kids *should* play in the mud with sticks and stones and all things mucky. Nature is there to be explored and nettles are there to sting. Let them learn about the world around them. And children should socialize, too. Get the neighbors' kids involved. Children teach each other and they are far less likely to be bored in the company of another child than they are with you. Safety is key, however. Watch from a distance—reclining on a picnic blanket if you can—and allow the little loves to run all that energy off. If they show a tiny piece of interest in anything, grab it and run with it!

- *Cook with them.* Line up a summer of recipes and sit back and watch the mayhem! Prepare for your kitchen to look like an explosion in a flour factory and for your stomach to have to grow a steel lining. But I have yet to find a child who doesn't relish making a pastry dinosaur for you to have for dinner. And how proud they are of that cheesy mud pie!

- *Go somewhere educational.* This can become pricey. But if boredom is setting in with weeks left of the summer, short trips may just save you. Go to the natural history museum, the science museum, the ancient monuments—anything that may spark an interest or a conversation. Make sure the place has toilets and a coffee shop, though. Mums and dads need refueling and children have bladders the size of a walnut.

- *Give them away.* Send them to summer school, if you can afford it. Otherwise, call in all grandmas and granddads, all aunties and uncles (real and honorary), all neighbors and friends, all sleep-over buddies! Getting other people involved will not only broaden your children's horizons; it will give you a chance to wander around the garden naked and get in touch with your deep natural side (if that's what your heart desires) without having to stop to make dinner. Always remember, however, that you may have to return the favor.

- *Return to childhood.* If you want to really enjoy the summer break, come back down from the parental heights and rediscover your inner child. Roll around on the grass and make dens; swing and climb if your knees are up to it. Eat ice cream; do something that feels good; laugh a lot. Look at the world through your children's eyes—with wonder and newness—instead of at the big pile of ironing that needs to be done. Just chuck those clothes in the cupboard and wear them creased. What does it really matter?

- *Get magical.* If your children show even a tiny glimmer of interest in what you do magically, encourage it! Help them create their own Book of Shadows. Discover the elements together. Help them craft their first wand and dance barefoot on the grass. Listen to music and revel in life and its forces. This is your opportunity to hand down your magical knowledge and rediscover the fun side of your beliefs.

Other ideas include arguing with them, ignoring them, and putting them to work. Watch television with them, if you can stand six weeks of kids' programs. Take them swimming. And of course, there's always that time-honored solution—just keep your fingers crossed. However you manage, good luck.

Fresh Fruit Time

July is the month when fruit comes to the forefront of the shopping basket—and about time too! I love fresh fruit, especially all the beautiful summer berries. But there is so much more you can do with our fruity friends than just eat them. Why not have a go at some of these ideas?

- *Freeze them.* Freeze whole bananas on a stick as a healthy banana ice-cream pop and use the peels to polish your shoes. It honestly works!

- *Dry them.* Dry out apple slices and use them to make a potpourri with cinnamon sticks and cloves.

- *Slice them.* A slice of fresh strawberry placed under the eyes reduces puffiness.

- *Bake them.* Bake orange peels in the oven for 10 minutes to remove stubborn cooking odors. Or steep them in white vinegar for a couple of weeks to create a wonderful all-purpose cleaner.

- *Mash them.* Make a homemade face mask by mixing a mashed peach with a tablespoon of honey and some oatmeal to a thick consistency. Apply and leave for 10 minutes, then rinse for beautiful skin.

- *Plant them.* Use the scooped-out skin of a mango to cultivate seeds. Just fill with compost and sprinkle in your seeds. Once the seeds have sprouted, the whole thing can be planted just as is to avoid disturbing the roots.

Gooseberry Fool with Butter-Balm Biscuits (serves 4)

Ingredients for gooseberry fool

250 g./9 oz. gooseberries, topped and tailed

3 tbsp. caster sugar

200 g./7 oz. Greek yogurt

2 tbsp. icing sugar

Zest of half a lemon

1 tsp. vanilla extract

200 ml./6.5 oz. double cream

Method for gooseberry fool

1. Put the gooseberries, lemon zest, and sugar in a pan with a splash of water. Heat gently, stirring, then bring to a simmer and cook until the fruit starts to burst.

2. Squash the gooseberries with a fork until pulpy. Pop in the fridge to cool.

3. Put the yogurt in a bowl and beat with the icing sugar and vanilla until smooth. Gently whisk in the cream until the mixture is thick, then stir in the gooseberry pulp.

4. Spoon into glasses or bowls to serve.

Ingredients for butter biscuits

115 g./4 oz. butter

85 g./3 oz. caster sugar

3 egg yolks

225 g./8 oz. plain/all-purpose flour

2 tbsp. lemon balm, chopped

Zest of half a lemon

Pinch of salt

Method for butter biscuits

1. Preheat the oven to 190°C/375°F.

2. Beat the butter and sugar together until soft, then mix in the egg yolks.

3. Using a spatula, gently fold in half of the flour and the salt. When evenly mixed, fold in the rest of the flour, lemon zest, and chopped lemon balm to form a soft dough. Cover and chill in the fridge.

4. On a lightly floured surface, roll out the dough thinly and cut into 18 circles with a pastry cutter.

5. Place on a baking tray and pop into the oven for 10 minutes, until light golden in color.

6. Leave to cool slightly on the baking tray, then transfer to a wire rack to cool completely.

This beautifully luxurious pudding is a family favorite at my house. It's something my mum always used to make when my brother and I were kids. Let's all grow and eat more gooseberries. They're delicious!

Witchy Ways to Celebrate July

- Decorate your home and altar with fragrant lavender and honeysuckle; light beeswax candles to honor the honey bees.

- Eat seasonal food outside. Have a picnic, leaving some food behind as an offering to the earth.

- Do something new with your magic. Work with different elements and spell ingredients, or cook a new recipe with love.

- Spell for the prosperity of other countries. Send healing and blessings out to the world.

- Spend time outside barefoot on the earth. Make a magic map of where you live and what's around you. If you have children, include them.

July Folklore

"St. Swithin's day, if thou dost rain, for forty days it shall remain."

"St. Swithin's day, if thou be fair, for forty days, twill rain nae mair!"

"If the first of July it be rainy weather, twill rain more or less for four weeks together."

Chapter Six

———◆———

AUGUST

It is the time to cut John Barleycorn dead,
His blood will spill all berries red.
We will bury him in the earth where he will rest for a year,
And he will spring up again next year with a shout and a cheer!

Foods at Their Best in August

Fruits and Vegetables

artichokes, aubergines, apricots, blackberries, bobby beans, buckler-leaf sorrel, beetroot, blueberries, broad beans, carrots, chard, cob nuts, coley, courgettes, cherries, cucumbers, figs, fennel, french beans, greengages, gooseberries, garlic, kohlrabi, loganberries, new potatoes, onions, peaches, potatoes, plums, rocket, runner beans, red currants, radishes, raspberries, sorrel, sweet corn, spinach, salad leaves, turnips, tomatoes, watercress

Seafood

brill, clams, cockles, cod, crab, crayfish, Dover sole, gray mullet, haddock, halibut, herring, John Dory, lobster, langoustines, lemon sole, monkfish, mackerel, nectarines, pollack, plaice, squid, scallops, sea bass, sea trout, sardines, salmon

Wild foods

black mustard, blackberry, cep, crab apples, early damsons, elderberries, field mushroom, giant puffball, gooseberry, grouse (august 12), hare, hazelnut, heather flowers, marsh samphire, rabbit, raspberry, rosehip, sea beet, sea purslane, venison, wild mushrooms, wild strawberry, wood pigeon, wild blackberries, wild mint

August Correspondences

- **Festival:** Lammas (Lughnasadh). The first harvest. Symbols include scythes and sickles, all grains, sheaves of wheat, honey, grapes, and wine.

- **Moon name:** Sturgeon Moon, after the fish that is most easily caught during this month. Other names include Corn Moon, Green Corn Moon, Lightning Moon, and Dog Days Moon.

- **Astrological signs:** Leo, July 21–August 20; Virgo, August 21–September 20.

- **Birthstones:** Peridot and sardonyx.

- **Nature spirits:** Crop and earth spirits.

- **Animals:** Horse and otter.

- **Birds:** Wood pigeon and swift.

- **Trees:** Hazel and elder.

- **Flowers:** Sunflower, cornflower, and harebell.

- **Herbs:** Lady's bedstraw, parsley, and basil.

- **Scents:** Sandalwood and heather.

- **Colors:** Gold and red.

- **Goddess:** Ceres.

- **Powers:** Reaping what you have sown; transformation and prosperity; letting go of regrets.

- **Other:** A time for carnivals and festivals.

Hot, beautiful, sunny August is here. The pinnacle of the summer, with long warm days of sunshine, warm balmy evenings, and a laid-back feel of relaxation. *Al fresco* dining is here as well, and maybe a lovely cool gin and tonic in the garden? Don't mind if I do! That is, of course, unless you have a child.

Then August tends to stretch out like a never-ending marathon of amusing the little monsters, complete panic, and financial ruin as you stave off the "we're bored" complaints and tackle the—horror of horrors—school uniform! Oh yes, every store sports big bright bold banners with "Back to School" scribed upon them. And you may as well just empty your purse as you reach the shop door! Shoes, socks, vests, and school bags; paper and pens and lunch boxes; gym kits and coats—you need to be a magician with money and have nerves of steel to deal with a fashion-conscious teenager who refuses any skirt but the completely inappropriate short, tight one!

Good luck if this is you. I have also served my time on this mission and do not miss the August uniform run at all. Hang in there. One day you realize that they are all grown up and you no longer dread August—and you have been liberated!

Lammas (Lughnasadh)

August is a clear example of how we live by the new calendar instead of the old. We look upon August as a time of summer. But it is, in fact, more aligned with the autumn, because the first harvests start this month. The festival of Lammas (loaf mass) is the start of the harvest, when we begin to reap what we have sown. The vegetable plot is abundant with yummy fruits and vegetables, and out in the fields, the golden expanses of wheat and corn are ready to be cut and baled. I have always thought that this is the time when the countryside looks its most alive. It is certainly the time when the roads and lanes are dominated by two new kinds of wildlife—the tractor and the combine harvester! Many an hour has been lost stuck behind one of these trundling machines. I remember one particularly bad August when I lived down a narrow country road and spent most of my time running out of the house to move my car because the harvester couldn't fit past it!

The first harvest marks the start of abundance and the celebration of the grain we have all come to depend on but tend take for granted as we pop down to the shop to buy a loaf of bread. But the first harvest is also a time of honoring our ancestors. Can you imagine how hard harvest time was for them, when the success of the crops meant the difference between life and death?

Grain is a symbol of death and rebirth, and the story of John Barleycorn is often told at this time. John Barleycorn is the living spirit within the corn. When the corn is cut down, he gives his life so that others may be fed and nourished by the grain. He is consumed in the form of bread and is reborn in the seed that is replanted. The cycle of death and rebirth is present in him.

The first and last sheaves of the harvest carry traditional and magical importance. Traditionally, the first sheaf was cut at dawn, the grain ground to make harvest bread, and the stalks made into beer to share with the community. The last sheaf was made into a corn dolly to be taken to the harvest festival and then kept in the home to ensure good luck and a successful harvest the following year. Often, the corn husks were made into a maiden. But in bad harvest years, it was fashioned as a crone. This corn dolly was always returned to the earth as a symbol of rebirth, either ploughed back into the fields or burned and the ashes scattered, usually when the first ploughing of the fields took place to plant a new crop.

Another name for this Wheel of the Year festival is Lughnasadh (pronounced *loo-nas-ad*), named for the Celtic god of craftsmanship, Lugh. This is the time of year when craft fairs and festivals still take place, so it is a wonderful time to use your old skills and learn new ones. This amazing time of the first harvest is also a time when we should let go of any regrets or habits we want to leave behind and give thanks for what we have reaped and for what we have. This simple ritual is a good way to combine the symbolic Lugh and his craftsmanship with the ritual release of regrets and with thanksgiving. If you know how to create a corn dolly, use your skill here. If, like me, you can't, these simple Lammas sticks will work beautifully well.

Simple Lammas Sticks

You will need:

Three sheaves of corn or three slim, small sticks

A needle

Three rosehips

Sit comfortably outside if you can. Pierce the three rosehips with a sharp needle to create a hole big enough to thread the sticks or corn sheaves through. Thread the rosehips onto the sheaves or sticks, one on each.

Hold the first one and focus on letting go of anything you regret from the last year. Focus all those regrets into the rosehip on the sheaf or stick, turning it in your hand as you push all those regrets into it. Then pick up the second stick and hold it in your hand. Focus on giving thanks to the world, to the Goddess and the God, and to all things that make your life what it is. Be thankful for any lessons learned or problems you have overcome in this year. Finally, pick up the third stick and hold it in your hand. Focus on all the good in your life and all the things that have come to fruition this year. Turn it over and over in your hands, imagining a bright light of positivity being pushed into it.

When you have worked with all the sticks, take the first one—the one full of regrets you wish to leave behind—and bury it. Imagine, as you do so, the earth turning all those regrets into positivity. Turn away from the regrets and don't look back as you leave. Then take the second stick—the one full of your thanks—and leave it somewhere special to you or cast it into a stream. As you let it go, imagine the thanks you have placed in it being sent out into the world to be heard. Finally, take the third stick home and place it somewhere prominent in your house or on your altar. Use this stick as your focus through any tough times, as a symbol of lessons learned and rewards gained. Return this back to the earth at the next harvest.

Sweet Lammas No-Knead Bread (1 med. loaf)

This is a great recipe to have up your sleeve at any time of the year, but particularly at harvest time. The hazelnuts should be ready to be foraged, and any seeds you use can symbolize the rebirth cycle.

Ingredients

250 g./9 oz. whole-meal flour

85 g./3 oz. all-purpose flour

1 tsp. baking soda

40 g./1.5 oz. brown sugar

70 g./2.5 oz. cold butter, cubed

175 g./6 oz. fresh figs, cut into pieces

100 g./3.5 oz. hazelnuts

300 ml./10 oz. buttermilk

Seeds and oats to decorate the top

Method

1. Preheat the oven to 180°C/ 350°F.

2. Butter a loaf tin.

3. In a bowl, mix the flours, baking soda, and sugar. Rub in the cold butter with your fingers.

4. Mix in the figs and hazelnuts, and add the buttermilk.

5. Mix with your hands to a sticky dough and place in the greased tin.

6. Roughly smooth out the top and sprinkle with oats and seeds.

7. Bake for 50 minutes in the center of the oven.

8. Leave to cool in the tin for 5 minutes, then turn out and let cool on a wire rack.

Serve this wonderful sweet bread sliced, with apples and cheese, or just with creamy butter. This makes a great offering for the Fae or for thanksgiving. Try different fruits and nuts to ring the changes, and turn any leftovers into bread pudding, or allow it to go stale and blitz it into crumbs as a tasty crunchy baked-fruit topping.

Your Home As Sanctuary

As a time of year when we tend to spend a lot of time around our homes, August is perfect for throwing open the windows and doors and focusing on our environment. We all look upon our homes as our sanctuaries, so we should, if we can, take some time to honor and bless them. I always try to bless my home when I do my general cleaning, but in August, with the fresh air and light streaming through the windows, it seems a logical time to do a whole-home blessing.

Blessing Your Home

Blessing the home is something that our ancestors did regularly, and there are so many ways in which you can do it. This is one of my favorites.

Open your windows and doors if you can and go to the heart of your home. If you are lucky enough to have a real fireplace or hearth, which was traditionally the center of the home, go there. More often these days, however, the heart of the home is the kitchen or living room. Use the place where your family seems to congregate the most.

Light a white candle for purity, and a cleansing incense like rosemary or sage. Focus on the flame of the candle. Imagine its light spreading throughout your home, touching every corner and illuminating it with positivity. Say some simple words, like:

Light of flame, dance for me,

Cleansing my home, so mote it be!

Then focus on the incense smoke as it swirls and mixes with the fresh air that is wafting in from outside. Imagine that the smoke is being carried to all the corners of your home, cleansing any negativity away. Say some simple words, like:

Swirling smoke, remove all fear

Cleanse and bless each corner here,

So mote it be!

If you can, carry the incense and candle into each room and hold them aloft, repeating your words. If you can't, just imagine their properties doing just that. When you feel that your blessing has worked, allow the candle to burn safely down or extinguish it with thanks. Take any incense to the front door and allow the smoke to waft over the outside of the door, imagining blessings being bestowed on all those who enter it. Finish with: "So mote it be!" when you feel the door has been blessed.

Protecting Your Home

The last ritual is a wonderfully simple and effective way to bless your home, but here are some other ways in which you can magically protect and bless the place where you live:

- *Blow bubbles.* I know it sounds mad, but what an enjoyable way to bless your home and get the little ones involved too! Pour the bubble mixture into a pretty bowl and, holding your hand over it, ask for it to be blessed with happiness and goodness. Then go outside and blow those blessings all around your home. (Just make sure you do it before you wash your windows. Mr. Hedgewitch once got a bit cross at all the bubble splatters across his clean panes. Not much happiness there!)

- *Float balloons.* This method of home blessing is great fun for the kids. Blow up balloons and float them up to touch the roof of the house to get your blessings up as far as you can. Be imaginative!

- *Sweep away negativity.* Use a broom that is reserved for just this task. A bundle of twigs tied with some cleansing herbs makes a great energy-clearing broom. Go around the house in a clockwise motion, sweeping out every room. End at the front door and sweep the negativity out with the words: "Be gone!"

- *Create a protective boundary.* Sprinkle the perimeter of your home with salt to enclose it in a protective circle. Ask that no negativity cross this boundary. You can also bury jasmine incense sticks at the four corners of your property for blessings and protection. Use herbs here too. Strong-smelling herbs are the best for dealing with negativity, so sage, pine, and mint are all great to use. Combine them with peace-giving herbs like lavender, hops, or chamomile to create a peaceful boundary.

- *Bless the threshold.* Focus some time on the entrance to your home. Your front door carries everything from outside over the threshold, so bless and protect it well. A pot of basil grown at the front door is a great way to do this. And wipe the door handle with lavender oil to touch everyone symbolically who enters with peace.

- *Inscribe your blessing.* Take a small dish of oil—any will do, but I like to use olive oil—and place your hand over it, asking that it be filled with the power of blessings. Then visit every window and door in your home and, with your finger dipped in the oil, inscribe a protective symbol on each. You can use a flame, a pentacle, a sun, a flower, or anything that represents blessings to you. This also works well when performed with herbal tea. Try chamomile for peace, lemon for cleansing, etc.

- *Beat the boundary.* This comes from an old British custom in which communities came together and beat the ground around the boundaries of the village with willow sticks that they called wands—and we know all about them, don't we! This was done to ensure that the village was blessed, and to drive out any negativity for the coming year. So grab a willow stick if you can— your broom will work just as well—and beat the ground around your home, saying:

Blessings in and evil out,
Protection gained, there is no doubt!

- *Leave offerings.* The spirits of your home and hearth need to be remembered too. Leave offerings of honey, cream, or cake to the Fae of your home and garden, thanking them for their presence in your household and asking them to bestow blessings upon it. Remember, they won't consume what you leave, but they will feast on the essence. So keep your offerings fresh and light a candle occasionally to honor them.

- *Hang blessings.* Make some little sachets with herbs and flowers to hang in your home. Basil is a wonderful herb to use for love and protection, but tailor your mix to what you want it to do. Keep your home in your mind as your create each sachet. Tie them with ribbons whose colors are associated with your spell and say the words: "So mote it be!" as you hang each one. You can also hang crystals in the windows to bounce their rainbow light around each room.

COLOR MAGIC

We all use and make decisions about color in our daily lives—what colors we wear, which paints we use, the cars we drive, the food we eat, even the shampoos we buy. A whole host of decisions we make every day are at least partly decided by color. Most people have a favorite color. Mine is purple, and most of my home is decorated in shades of this color. Even my cloak is a beautiful shade of heather. It is a color that I am comfortable with. You will have your own favorite shade that features prominently in your life—and hopefully you have an understanding partner if your favorite color is acid green or Barbie pink!

The use of color can really enhance your magic and spell work, because each color lends its own energy and its associations to your spells and rituals. There are many ways to include color magic in your work—from candle magic to knot magic, from spell bags to plant magic. In fact, all of your magic will be greatly enhanced by your own knowledge of which colors work in which ways. I believe that there is no right or wrong color chart; what works for one will not necessarily work for all. If a certain color means a certain thing to you, who's to say that you're wrong and some impersonal chart is right? For example, when you think of the Goddess, do you see her as white? Silver? Gold? Blue? Who's to tell you which is the right color?

The right color is the one with which you feel confident and comfortable working. And the right colors are the ones you can remember. If you want to create a spell spontaneously, you don't want to have to go looking for a color-correspondence chart to find out which color works in a certain way. You have to trust what's in your heart and work in a way that is true to you. I suggest you create your *own* color chart in your Book of Shadows. Spend some time thinking about what each color evokes for you and write it down. If you need some guidelines, below is the basic list I use in my own magic. Maybe it will give you a starting point or help you add to your own list. If you already work with color, try exploring some of the more intricate shades of each color to expand your catalog.

White: protection and purity; use in all magic as a universal color

Black: to absorb negativity and spirit contact; for banishing spells

Yellow: confidence and growth; for harmony spells

Red: strength and passion; for power spells

Blue: health and patience; for awareness spells

Purple: peace and meditation; for blessing spells

Pink: relaxation and friendship; for love spells

Green: nature and Fae magic; for wealth spells

Brown: earth and animals; for grounding spells

Orange: luck and vitality; for strength spells

Silver: the Goddess and the moon; for balance spells

Gold: the God and the sun; for power spells

Every color, of course, has varying shades—from pastel to deep or bright. Make your list as simple or as complicated as you like. A good way to build your own list is to have someone read off colors to you and you say the first thing that comes into your head that you associate with each color. That way, you will know that you are working with what's true to your heart and with something that you will remember.

The ways in which you can use color in your magic are as varied as the colors themselves. Once you have your own color chart, there are many ways to incorporate each color into your magical workings. Here are a few of my favorites.

Knots

Start gathering a supply of varied cords, embroidery threads, or yarns. These will give you a wonderful basis for knot or cord magic. Select the color cord you wish to represent your spell and sit quietly. Focus your intent into the cord. When you are ready, start creating knots in the cord to create your spell. When you are done making knots, place your cord on your altar, or bury or burn it to complete the spell. I like to use wording like this as I make my knots:

By knot of one, the spell's begun.

By knot of two, it becomes true.

By knot of three, so shall it be.

By knot of four, it binds it more.

By knot of five, spell comes alive.

By knot of six, the spell shall fix.

By knot of seven, up to the heavens.

By knot of eight, it shall not wait.

By knot of nine, spell shall be mine.

So mote it be!

Ribbons

Start a collection of ribbons. It's amazing how these seem to materialize once you actively look for them. The best way I have found to build up my collection is to cut out the hanging ribbons from old clothes. These come in a variety of colors and are just the right length for spell-bag work.

Once you have selected and charged the ingredients for your spell, select the appropriate color ribbon and hold it between your palms. Focus on the color strengthening your spell work. When you're ready, tie the spell bag closed with the ribbon, saying:

Color strengthen this spell for me,

Enclose the magic within.

Success with your help I now decree,

A web of magic I spin.

So mote it be!

Focus

I love to work focus magic, especially for healing. For this, all you need is plain paper and some colored pencils. Sit somewhere comfortable and clear your mind of everything other than the healing you wish to send to someone or something.

When you have a clear image in your mind, select the colored pencils that you feel represent your image and begin to draw it. Draw whatever you feel represents your spell—for healing, a candle and flame; for nature, flowers; whatever comes to you. Use your colors to bring the healing really alive. You don't have to be a great artist for this; just draw what's in your heart. Fill the paper with your colors.

When you have finished, you can use this as your focus anytime you want to work on that spell. When your spell has been successful, burn your paper and return the ashes to the earth for recycling. I find this kind of magic wonderful for children to perform. They naturally get very absorbed when drawing, giving it their full focus and intent.

Flowers

Flowers give you a wonderful opportunity to work color magic. Select your flowers by color to create a vase tailored to your spell. Place this vase of flowers on your altar if you have one, and light a candle of a corresponding color in front of it. Watch as the flame illuminates the flowers' colors in the vase and imbues them with your spell.

Once your candle has burned down, take your flowers outside and lay them around the base of a tree. Focus on the colors surrounding the tree and see your spell carried up through the branches and out into the world. If you are spelling for someone else, give them one of the flowers as a token of your spell. Otherwise, leave your flowers as an offering. As you watch the candle burn, you can say a few simple words, like:

Blooms of color, come to dance and play,

Spell spring to life upon this day.

So mote it be!

Witches' Bottles

Create a witch's bottle containing colored threads and crystals. Write your spell on colored paper, roll it up, and place it in the bottle. Seal it with the appropriate colored wax (simple coloring crayons are great for this). Bury your bottle outside to complete your spell. Or if you are working a spell for the home, tuck it away in a cupboard.

Empowerment

Color can also be used magically to imbue a location with its power. So why not have a go at introducing some color magic to your home? There are many everyday objects and materials you can use to bring color energies into your simple spells and rituals.

- *Fruits*. Place a bowl of citrus fruits on your kitchen table to cleanse and brighten the atmosphere.

- *Flowers*. Add drawings or paintings of flowers to bring their colorful essences in all year round.

- *Plants*. Place green plants in a belligerent teenager's bedroom to soothe and calm.

- *Spices*. Place dried brown spices in a bowl in the living room for a grounding essence and a wonderful scent.

- *Ribbons*. Use plaited ribbons as curtain tiebacks and change them on festival days to represent the turning of the Wheel.

- *Decorations*. Change a dull space magically by redecorating it with colors attuned to your desires.

- *Mirrors*. Place mirrors opposite windows to reflect the outside.

Have fun experimenting with colors. Grow in confidence using them, and your magic will grow in strength as well!

Raspberry Mint Meringue Pie (serves 8)

This recipe is a novel take on the classic lemon meringue pie we all love. The green flecks of mint in the meringue and the pinky-red of the raspberry filling are just the thing to represent summer on a plate. They are a wonderful way to work with color in your food—and yummy too! This does need more preparation time than some recipes, but it is always worth cooking this with love and serving it up at a family barbecue.

Ingredients for the pastry

150 g./5 oz. all-purpose flour, plus extra to dust

25 g./1 oz. caster sugar

75 g./2.5 oz. butter, cubed and chilled

1 large egg yolk

Ingredients for the filling

800 g./28 oz. fresh raspberries

5 tbsp. corn flour

100–125 g./3.5–4.5 oz. golden caster sugar, to taste

2 tbsp. lemon juice

5 large egg yolks

60 g./2 oz. butter

Ingredients for the meringue

3 large egg whites

175 g./6 oz. golden caster sugar

3 tbsp. fresh mint, chopped

Method for the pastry

1. Preheat the oven to 190°C/375°F.

2. Add the flour and the sugar to a bowl and rub in the butter.

3. Add the egg yolk and a tbsp. of cold water and bring the ingredients together to form a dough. Wrap and place in the fridge for 30 minutes to rest.

4. Roll out the pastry on a floured surface and use it to line a pie plate. Line with baking paper and fill with baking beans.

5. Place on a baking sheet and bake for 15 minutes. Remove the beans and paper and bake for another 10 minutes, or until golden. Set aside to cool.

6. Reduce the oven temperature to 180°C/350°F.

Method for the filling

1. Purée the raspberries in a blender, then pass the purée through a sieve to remove the seeds. You should end up with 675–700 ml./23–24 oz. of purée. Pour the purée into a saucepan.

2. In a bowl, mix the corn flour with 100 g./3.5 oz. sugar, the lemon juice, and 1 tbsp. water to give a paste. Stir into the purée.

3. Place over a medium heat and cook, stirring until just boiling. Cook for 1 minute, stirring continuously until thickened. Taste and add the extra sugar if you like it a bit sweeter.

4. Remove from the heat and beat in the egg yolks and butter. Cool slightly, then pour into the pie shell and chill for 30 minutes.

Method for the meringue

1. Whisk the egg whites to soft peaks in a large bowl. Gradually whisk in the sugar, until you have a stiff, shiny meringue. Gently fold in the chopped mint.

2. Pile the meringue on top of the raspberry filling, swirling with a palette knife to get some peaks.

3. Bake for 10 minutes, or until the meringue is pale golden. Serve immediately!

Food Magic

Okay, for however brief a time, the sun is shining and it looks as if we may have a few days of summer left. Now listen. What do you hear? Is it the crash of waves on a beach? The glugging of wine into a glass? The gentle rustle of the leaves in a summer breeze? I bet it's none of the above. The sound you hear is likely the tuneless melody of the ice cream man. Oh yes, we've all heard it—that terrible rendition of the *Entertainer*, or *Raindrops Keep Falling on My Head!* My children, who had selective hearing most of the time, could hear the ice cream man streets away. When they did, they ran inside at top speed—like Lisa and Bart Simpson—with hands outstretched for money and cleared out my purse in a hurry! Their prize? That wonderful, magical ice cream—the only thing that seems to hit the spot on a hot summer day—apart from gin and tonic. Now where did I put that?

That to me is what food magic is all about—that amazing feeling of the right food, in the right situation, at the right time. Food magic can be as simple or complicated as you like. But it is something that never grows old. Nor can you ever know everything there is to know about it, so you can always learn new ways in which to combine foods and make them magical. Food is a magical tool that can create a powerful spell, and cooking is the most powerful ritual you can perform. It's alchemy! Every food contains energy, and if you prepare that food with love and intent, you are performing magic—an old, sacred magic that you can practice and hone every day in your very own kitchen.

So if you want to perform food magic, where do you start? I think there are a few key points in food magic that are the same no matter what you are creating. Here are a few tips to give your kitchen magic added power:

- *Start with clean hands.* This doesn't mean just washed clean. It means clean from any other energy you may have picked up in your day. So when you wash your hands before you cook, focus on washing away all negativity, as well as any germs. Clean your hands carefully and thoroughly, really focusing on the task.

- *Keep your goal in mind.* Oh boy, does this one take some practice! It is hard to leave your 1,001 worries at the kitchen door. But only true focus will produce a pure result. Ban all idle chitchat and all the "Mum, where's my . . ." interruptions from your time in the kitchen so that you can really concentrate on your spell. The warning "Do not disturb unless it's an emergency" should be instilled in all who dare to enter!

- *Work with care.* Concentrate on doing the best job you know how every time you work your food magic. Slap-dash cooking is not the order of the day; sloppily chucking ingredients together will produce a chaotic spell.

- *Stir clockwise (deosil) for positivity.* This was done by our ancestors as well, because they thought they were stirring in the direction of the path of the sun. If you stir counterclockwise (widdershins) by mistake, bang your spoon nine times on your bowl or pan, and then go back to stirring clockwise. The nine bangs will chase the negativity away.

- *Use symbols and shapes.* Draw a symbol with your spoon in the bottom of your pan before cooking. Cut out shapes and symbols of pastry or dough. Arrange food in patterns that link to your spell. Hearts are great for love magic, a flame for protection, a star for health—use whatever speaks to you.

- *Think about your foods.* Each food has different associations, different powers, and different uses. Plan what you are going to cook and find out as much as possible about the properties of each ingredient. Think about how your ingredients will combine together. If you feel strongly that a particular food carries the essence you need to include, use it! Trust your instincts.

- *Stock an herb larder.* Herbs are the key to food magic because they have such strong energies and powers and can be used so easily. The power of herbal magic was well-known to our ancestors and we can tap into that power today. Learn about one herb's properties and uses before you go on to the next. Use fresh and dried varieties and feel the different powers they lend to your food. Grow herbs on your windowsill or buy them dried from the shop, but don't forget to charge any herb you use before cooking with it.

Witchy Ways to Celebrate August

- Decorate your home and altar with symbols of the harvest—apples, berries, and corn. A simple bowl of oats works well as a focus. Use both summer and autumnal colors in your flowers and burn basil, lavender, and cinnamon incense.

- Bake a loaf of bread using local flour if you can, and share it with your family, friends, and neighbors. Leave some out as an offering to the Fae and as thanks for the harvest.

- Notice the seasonal changes that are coming by walking in the sunshine and watching out for the changes in the air that herald autumn.

- Expand your magic by using color or food magic to create a thanksgiving feast with the local bounty of produce that is available.

- Try making a simple corn dolly, or learn a skill or craft.

- Write down your regrets and thanks in your Book of Shadows to record your Lammas journey.

- Start to preserve the harvest by making jams, chutneys, or pickles so you can have a taste of summer later in the year.

August Folklore

"The hottest days of the year are often found in August."

"Dry August and warm doth harvest no harm."

"If the first August be warm, then winter will be white and long."

Chapter Seven

September

This is the season for blackberry picking

Watch your fingers on the thorns for they stick in!

Gather together all that has grown

And bring it back to bake at home.

Foods at Their Best in September

Fruits and Vegetables

apples, apricots, bilberries, butternut squash, blackberries, beetroot, blueberries, cabbages, chard, chicory, cob nuts, celeriac, cucumbers, figs, fennel, greengages, garlic, kohlrabi, leeks, new potatoes, onions, potatoes, plums, pumpkin, pears, Swiss chard, sweet corn, spinach, turnips, tomatoes, watercress

Seafood

brill, clams, cockles, cod, crab, Dover sole, flounder, gray mullet, halibut, herring, lemon sole, lobster, langoustines, mackerel, mussels, pollack, oysters, plaice, sea bream, skate, squid, scallops, sea bass, salmon, turbot, whelks, winkles

Wild Foods

beech nuts, bilberry, black mustard, blackberry, crab apples, cherry plums, comfrey, dandelion roots, damsons, elderberries, guinea fowl, grouse, hare, hawthorn berries, hawthorn, hazelnut, heather flowers, hops, horseradish, Jack-by-the-hedge, juniper, mallard, nettles, partridge, poppy, rowan berries, rosehips, marsh samphire, sea plantain, sea beet, sea blight, sea purslane, teal, truffles, venison, wild rabbit, wild mushrooms, wild duck, wild mint, wild plums, wild strawberry, wood pigeon

(Wow! A larder full of free foods this month!)

September Correspondences

- *Festival*: Mabon. The second harvest. Symbols include the corn dolly, bread, cornucopia, nuts, acorns, and leaves.

- *Moon name*: Harvest Moon. Other names include Singing Moon, Barley Moon, and Corn Moon.

- *Astrological signs*: Virgo, August 21–September 20; Libra, September 21–October 20.

- *Birthstones*: Sapphire and lapis lazuli.

- *Nature spirits*: Trooping fairies and gnomes.

- *Animals*: Dogs and corn snakes.

- *Birds*: Chiffchaff and birds of prey.

- *Trees*: Sycamore and chestnut.

- *Flowers*: Marigold, dahlias, and loosestrife.

- *Herbs*: Chamomile and oregano.

- *Scents*: Cinnamon and sage.

- *Colors*: Orange, deep red, and brown.

- *Goddess*: Modron.

- *Powers*: A time for protection, security, and balance in all things; returning to the earth.

- *Other*: Harvest festivals, Michaelmas Day, Goose Day, Holy Rood Day, and back to school—hurrah!

September comes rolling in with a wonderful scent, crisp leaves, cooling air, and bonfire smoke. This is my favorite time of year, when Mother Nature dons her most spectacular robes and treats us all to an amazing fashion show.

I think another reason that September holds such magic is that it's back-to-school time. You have survived the seemingly endless school holidays. You and your kids are intact and ready to be parted once again. The little angels, complete with shiny uniforms and lunch boxes, are bundled back to education and you can breathe a sigh of relief and give yourself a well-deserved pat on the back. My top tip for back-to-school season is to make sure you have the morning of the first day free. Book time off if you have to, and hit a coffee shop! Order an indulgent coffee and sit in the adult world for a while; sip coffee and congratulate yourself on a job well done. You can feel rightly smug; surviving the kids' break is no mean feat!

I think my love of September comes from going back to school when I was a child. The walk to school took me through the trees with their changing leaves and across the school field. The grass was wet with morning dew and the mist wafted around the borders of the field. All across the grass, a network of tiny delicate spiderwebs sparkled with fine droplets of dew. It looked as if the fairies had been weaving blankets under which to sleep. I loved to walk among these threads, imagining the sleeping Fae, tired from their night of spinning. I could have taken the path to school, but the magical field always drew me across. Wet feet for the rest of the day seemed a small price to pay!

September brings us many gifts as nature starts to wind down the year. This is the time when we celebrate the second harvest, the autumn equinox, and the festival of Mabon. We all love a celebration, and this is a particularly abundant one, with the crops already in and the fruit and autumn vegetable harvest taking hold. It is again a time of balance—around September 21—and the day is once again equal in length to night.

Mabon is all about sharing and giving thanks—the original harvest festival time when communities came together to share food and honor the Wheel of the Year. They gave thanks and blessings for the bounty of the earth provided to them before the longer cold nights took hold. So now's a great time to pop round to a neighbor and have a cuppa, a natter, and an exchange of garden bounty.

I imagine that most of us participated in harvest festivals at school—in the U.K., they are still part of the school year. Everyone takes an item of food into school to give to the elderly of the community. I have always given a tin of some description from the back of the cupboard—usually soup or beans with a layer of dust around the top. But there was always one classmate who turned up with an overflowing basket put together by his or her mum and intended to put us all to shame!

I remember one particular thanksgiving service I attended at the church next to the school when my girls were young. The church was freezing and it was the last place I wanted to be. But you know what it's like; you have to look willing! Myself and Mr. Hedgewitch sat on the unforgiving, cold church pews, waving at the girls, who were sitting at the front waiting to perform their harvest song and not concentrating on the service at all. The vicar was a stern-looking individual who, with an extremely boring voice, told us all how we should be giving thanks. But he didn't sound thankful at all. He then proceeded to ask the children for things that they associated with harvest time. One small boy, who couldn't have been more than five, put up his hand and said "vest," because it was part of the word "harvest." The vicar told him that was ridiculous and moved on to the next child.

Mr. Hedgewitch was furious. Why wasn't a vest something associated with the harvest? Surely at harvest time it gets colder and you need a vest to work outside? He spent most of the rest of the service complaining of this fact to me in whispered tones. Most indignant, he was. And why is it that you have to whisper in a church when it's supposed to be a place of thanksgiving and worship? I've never understood that.

Something else happened in that dreary service that I will never forget, as it put me firmly on my path. I looked at all those innocent little faces—ages between five and ten—as they were told to recite the Lord's Prayer. Now, I was brought up attending a Christian school, as were most of these kids, and that prayer was deeply ingrained in my memory. But at this particular service, I realized as I looked at my own children reciting that familiar prayer that they didn't understand the words they were saying. They were just repeating something parrot-fashion. And the words themselves sent shivers down my spine—"forgive us our trespasses, as we forgive those who trespass against us." Those beautiful children surely had not trespassed in a way to require forgiveness! I realized, at that moment, that words have power only when they are fully understood and spoken with focus on their meaning. You can never fully give anything of yourself unless you really feel the words you are saying and they resonate with you. Certainly, looking at those children that day was a massive wake-up call for me. And it was the last time I attended any church service.

Our ancestors used Mabon as a time to take stock of what they had achieved in the year—how much food they had that could be stored for the coming dark time—and to give their thanks to the earth as the soil started to die. Today, in a time when food is readily available all year round, we probably all take for granted that the winter will be fine. But can you imagine how it must have been if the harvest was poor and winter was coming? It was a matter of life and death, literally!

In September, as the world around us slows and dies, it is a time to retreat inward. As the Goddess becomes the Crone, it is a good time to give thanks, not only for what we have that's good, but also for the pain and suffering that teaches us valuable lessons and brings balance to our lives. Without the darkness, there would be no light; without sadness, how would we ever know joy? Mabon is a wonderful time for us to consider our inner balance and enjoy the fruits of our own toil throughout the year. It is a time to consider what we have harvested and what we have learned.

A lovely thing to do at this time of year is to make a ritual collage. After all, there is a wealth of things you can use, with all the fruits, nuts, and leaves around you now. This is a great way to include the kids, too. But make sure you do the sticking and gluing with them. And remember that magic is supposed to be full of joy!

Mabon Collage Ritual

You will need:

Collected natural items

A piece of paper

Flour and water, mixed to a thick paste

A candle

First, collect the materials for your collage—leaves in different shades, bark and twigs, seeds and nuts. Small stones and flowers work well too—anything that appeals to the eye. Once back home, mix some flour (any will do) with water to create a thick natural glue.

Light a candle at the table on which you will work. Place a piece of paper in front of you to represent yourself at the start of the year. Spend a few moments thinking about the balance of this time of year. Think about reaping what you have sown. Focus on what the aspects of light and dark in your life have taught you.

When you are ready, start to create your picture, gluing the pieces in place on the paper with the flour glue. As you do this, focus on obtaining a balance in your design—a balance of color and texture, of light and dark. Spend time creating your work and stay focused on balance. When you finish your design, leave it to dry for a few minutes. Allow your candle to burn down or blow it out with thanks.

You can do several things with your picture—display it with thanks as a reminder of the balance in your life, or bury or burn it with thanks as an offering. If you chose to display it, remember to take it down at the spring equinox.

PRESERVING FOOD

Our ancestors spent an awful lot of their time focused on food. And that's not really surprising, because they didn't have a supermarket just down the road, nor did they have a freezer to rummage around in. Today, we are so fortunate that the most we have to think about food is to decide what we are going to have for dinner tonight. For our ancestors, planning meals was done in advance—not a day in advance, but months in advance! How on earth, we wonder, did they cope? Well, it was all in the preparation. If a family stored the harvest correctly, it could keep them going through the winter. If they didn't, it could mean certain starvation. No pressure there!

Throughout the ages, with more advanced and modern technologies, the storage of food has become something we all take for granted. I think this has disconnected us from what we eat. Our ancestors had no fridges or freezers, so the storage of food must have been foremost in their minds. My grandmother had thirteen children. I have absolutely no idea how she coped without a fridge or a freezer, and with rationing around in the 1940s, too. What a nightmare it must have been!

Today, preserving food at home is not a concern for us. But I am a strong believer in connecting with what we eat, in as many ways as possible. I am not for one minute suggesting that we all throw out our fridges; we should embrace them and give them big squidgy cuddles just for being in our homes. And I am certain that our ancestors would have embraced and clung to the technologies we now have if they had had them. What I am suggesting is that we at least try to keep some of the old techniques alive to hand down to the next generation should they want or need them. I want us to have a better understanding of the work and love that can go into preserving our own harvest.

Preserving food is a real magical act; it shows reverence for what you are eating. If you have a massive vegetable plot, you probably automatically do a lot of preserving, because crops tend to be ready all at the same time. But even if you just have a few strawberry plants, preserving their fruit is a wonderful way to connect with it and keep that flavor of the harvest going through the winter months. Here are a few preserving methods you can use:

- *Drying.* The most ancient method of food preservation is a wonderful way to preserve herbs and spices. Hang them in small bunches of five or so stems in a warm, dark, airy place.

- *Freezing.* Blanch vegetables in boiling water for a few minutes, then cool and freeze them in bags. Freeze soft fruit by laying it out on a tray so each piece freezes individually. Then bag and label.

- *Salting.* This condiment can be used to preserve meat or fish.

- *Smoking.* Many cultures in many times have used smoke to preserve meat, fish, and cheeses.

- *Crystalizing.* Use sugar to preserve fruits in a syrup or to crystalize peels, ginger, etc. You can also use it to make jams and jellies.

- *Canning or bottling.* This preserves cooked foods in jars or tins.

- *Pickling.* Foods placed in vinegar, brine, or alcohol can be preserved for long periods of time.

- *Jugging.* This is a traditional method of preserving meat and game in a gravy, stewing it, and then storing it in a tightly closed jug.

- *Potting and confit.* Potting uses a layer of fat to make a seal on top of the food; confit is meat cooked in fat, traditionally goose fat.

- *Burial.* Storing food underground, traditionally potatoes and cabbages, can preserve them over the winter months.

- *Dry storage.* Store fruit and vegetables in layers of straw in a cool dry place, with the pieces not touching each other.

When you preserve your own food, you are hands-on during the whole process, so it's a good way to personalize your food. Experiment with new flavors and ingredients, or try a new method of preserving and see how it works for you. One of my favorite ways of preserving is to make jam and chutney. This is fairly simple and provides you with yummy treats all through the year. Here is one of my favorite recipes.

Autumn Chili Chutney

This easy-to-make preserve holds bursts of flavor and textures and brings you the colors of autumn in a jar. It keeps, unopened in the fridge, for up to two years—once opened, for around a month.

Ingredients

800 g./28 oz. butternut squash, cubed

2 red onions, chopped

225 g./8 oz. mango, cubed

1 orange, juiced and rind finely grated

400 g./14 oz. sugar

600 ml./20 oz. cider vinegar

½ tsp. turmeric

1 tsp. dried chili flakes

1 tbsp. coriander seeds

1 tbsp. salt

115 g./4 oz. flaked almonds

Method

1. Place the sugar and vinegar in a heavy-bottomed pan and heat gently, stirring occasionally until the sugar has dissolved.

2. Add all the remaining ingredients to the pan, except for the almonds.

3. Return the pan to the heat and slowly bring to a boil.

4. Reduce the heat and simmer the mixture gently for 45 minutes, stirring frequently until the chutney has reduced and no liquid remains.

5. Remove from the heat and stir in the flaked almonds.

6. Spoon into warm, sterilized jars and seal.

This wonderfully fragrant chutney works really well when served with curries or cheeses. Stir a spoonful into your gravy to lift the flavor, or turn it into a tangy dip for crudités by stirring a few spoonsful through plain yogurt. If you can bear to wait, it tastes even better after maturing for a month or so!

Earth Magic

As we go through September, the focus all around us seems to be with the earth. Fields are now bare, with the harvest brought in. The plants that flowered and gave us beauty from spring through summer are dying back. The earth is cooling and returning to its slumber.

Earth is one of the four elements with which we work. Earth sits in the north of the circle and, through its yearly cycles, really represents the turning of the Wheel. Earth magic can be grounding magic—a magic of change or a celebration of life. The earth is a nurturing force, solid and stable beneath our feet. She is Mother Earth, a mother to us all; we walk upon her every day, and return to her at the end of our lives.

The earth element can be represented as soil, salt, sand, rocks, or stones, so you can easily place it on your altar or in your home. Working with earth magic will also connect you to the earth Fae—the elves, brownies, and goblins that walk the land with us, in and between earth realms. So whenever you work with earth, always remember to include an offering or blessing to these spirit folk. They can be extremely mischievous and love nothing more than to trick us. Best keep them happy, eh?

Walking the path that we do, we probably connect with earth magic quite often. You know—when you stop and look at a view, or touch a tree, or smile at a flower. Here is a grounding earth-magic ritual that can be used to connect you solidly back to the earth. It can be really useful at those times when you feel that you're just all over the place. And if you've had to take some time away from your path, this ritual can help place you firmly back on it.

Connecting Ritual

Go outside and find somewhere quiet to sit. Take bread, water, and a small candle with you. You can go to the countryside or a park, or just sit in your own garden. Sit quietly with one hand placed on the ground and the other placed over your heart. Close your eyes.

Breathe deeply and slowly, and become aware of your own heartbeat. Focus on its rhythm. With your hand on the ground, visualize the heartbeat of Mother Earth pulsing through your hand. Imagine that heartbeat flowing up to your own heart, synchronizing both heartbeats into one.

In a soft voice, chant the simple words "We are one" to the rhythm of the heartbeats. Chant the words over and over, until you feel completely at one with the earth. When you have done this, ask that, when you open your eyes, you be shown the beauty of Mother Earth afresh to carry with you when you leave.

Open your eyes and look around you. Take note of any wildlife that may have come close. Look at the wonder around you as if you are seeing it for the first time. Light your small candle in honor of Mother Earth and focus on the light of the flame. See it spreading across the world, connecting you to all things.

Nourish yourself with the bread and water you brought with you. As you do so, imagine feeding and watering all of Mother Earth through your connection to her. Extinguish the candle with thanks, and leave some bread and water behind as an offering to any earth Fae spirits.

TRADITIONS

Traditions, the dictionary tells us, are long-held beliefs or behaviors passed down within a group or society that hold special meaning or significance. Yawn. What a boring definition! These days, the most important group most of us belong to is made up of our family and friends. So I expect there are times throughout the year when you and your family and friends get together to honor your own beliefs and activities with traditional celebrations or meals. Most families do.

The traditions of our ancestors tended to be all about the turning of the Wheel of the Year. They centered around crops and agriculture, and around the sun and the seasons. My main tradition tends to focus on when the Yule chocolates come out of the cupboard for the season. And it drives me mad that, even in September, the shops are already brimming with all things Christmas. Honestly, you can't move for tinsel out there in the aisles! This induces in me a feeling of complete panic, as though time were running away far too fast and if I don't buy that wrapping paper now, it'll all be gone, never to be found again!

Oh yes—traditions. Sorry, I was rambling again.

Every family has its own traditions that they honor throughout the year. But I think it's kind of important to stop and think about the traditions that have been handed down to us and then to think about making our own. After all, traditions have to start somewhere! Making your own magical traditions based on the Wheel of the Year can really give continuity to your journey and keep you connected to the tide of the seasons. Your traditions don't have to be big or flashy—just something simple. What you make for a meal to celebrate the festivals, or choosing a certain color candle to light can become traditions if you do them regularly. Magical traditions can be carried throughout your home as well. In the same way that you put up a tree around Yule, you can traditionally decorate your home in tune with the Wheel of the Year. And this has the added bonus of tailoring your environment to your magic.

At this time of Mabon, I like to string brightly colored leaves along colored ribbons to hang in the kitchen window. What makes it traditional is that it's something I do every year. I also get out and about in the hedgerows for the traditional blackberry-picking. All those little black jewels, ripe and plump from the sun, are just crying out to be picked and eaten. When I was little, blackberry picking was a tradition that most people did every year. Why have people stopped? I go to the supermarket and feel like crying when I see people buying blackberries in a plastic carton, when down the road they are free and fresh!

Mabon is also the easiest time to bring the outside in, with all of nature putting on one last show before winter. So, if you can, start your own tradition of decorating your home every autumn, even if it's just in a small way. And include your family in your new traditions if you can. If you do, there is a good chance that your traditions will be carried on and handed down. And your family will start to learn a little about what you do and why. Mr. Hedgewitch doesn't follow the same path that I do, but he is familiar with what I believe, mainly because I try to follow my own traditions throughout the year. Oh, and because I never stop talking! He says he doesn't listen, but some of it must get through, even if only by osmosis!

Here is a recipe that I make every year around Mabon. If you like it, maybe you can make it a part of your own Mabon tradition.

Wisdom Toads (serves 4)

These little adapted toads-in-the-hole are affordable and easy to make. The sage can be used for wisdom and goes beautifully with the pork sausages and apples. Mabon wouldn't be the same without them in my house!

Ingredients

8 good-quality pork sausages

100 g./3.5 oz. plain/all-purpose flour

300 ml./10 oz. milk

2 eggs

2 apples, sliced

4 tsp. whole-grain mustard

2 tsp. oil

8 sage leaves, charged for wisdom

Method

1. Preheat the oven to 220°C/425°F. Brush 8 cups of a muffin tin with the oil.

2. Carefully brown the sausages in a frying pan. Remove and set aside.

3. Sift the flour into a mixing bowl and season with salt and pepper.

4. In a jug, whisk together the milk, mustard, and egg until combined.

5. Gradually pour the milk mixture into the flour, mixing into a smooth batter.

6. Place the greased muffin tray into the oven to get it really hot.

7. Cut the sausages in half, then remove the muffin tin from the oven.

8. Place 2 halves of sausage, apple slices, and a sage leaf in each muffin section. Pour the batter over them.

9. Bake in the oven for 20 minutes, until risen and golden.

Serve hot from the oven, two per person, with mashed potatoes, peas, and gravy. How lovely to use the magical apple in something other than dessert—although I *am* partial to a pudding, as my tight jeans groaning at the seams can attest!

THE MAGICAL APPLE

Mabon brings the apple harvest, so this is a good time to have a look at this most magical of fruits. Legend has it that this sacred fruit originally came from the mythical Isle of Avalon, which is thought to be Glastonbury in Somerset. If you ever get a chance to visit there, you will see that it is awash with apple trees—and they make a cracking good cider there too! When cut horizontally across, the apple carries within it the sign of a pentacle, so is thought to be a secret way of telling someone you are a witch.

Apples are used for two main reasons in magic—for love and as food for the dead. Quite different uses, don't you think? For the love side of things, apples can be shared so that both lovers bite from one fruit. You can carve initials into them and then eat them or bury them. You can use them to foretell a lover's name. If you peel an apple in one long strip and let the peel drop to the floor, it will fall into the shape of the initial of your future lover. On the other hand, apples can be used to provide food for those departed. Pile them on the altar at Mabon, then bury them at Samhain to sustain the spirits of the dead through the winter, so they can be reborn in the spring.

There are many legends attached to apples. One says that you have to rub an apple before eating it to drive away evil spirits; if you don't, you are challenging the devil. Another says that if you win at apple bobbing, you will be next to get married or be blessed by the Goddess. Eating an apple is also said to open the realms of the Fae. And we've all heard the one that claims that an apple a day keeps the doctor away! Whether you eat your apple or use it to spell cast, it truly is the most magical of fruits. I think my favorite apple proverb is from Wales: A seed hidden in the heart of an apple is an orchard invisible! Just about sums it up, don't you think!

Apple Empowerment Spell

You will need:

    An apple

    A sharp knife

    A candle

First, light your candle. Then, with a sharp knife, cut the apple horizontally to reveal the pentacle inside. Tip each half of the apple upside down and tap gently to remove the seeds. Lay the halves of the apple, pentacle side up, next to each other in front of the candle.

Hold the apple seeds in your cupped hands and focus on the magic inside the seed—how, from a small seed, the apple tree grows. Imagine that you are the seeds—growing and blossoming on your path. Empower the seeds with your energy; trust that it is being absorbed into them. When you are ready, put the seeds down and carefully pick up the candle.

Drip a few drops of candle wax onto one of the pieces of apple, covering the pentacle. While the wax is still liquid, place a few of the seeds in the center of the pool of wax. Carefully drip more wax on top of the seeds to enclose them in the wax. Place the other apple half on top. Hold the apple in your hands and focus on the power within. Simply say:

Power of apple, fruit, seed, and tree,
Empower my journey and strengthen me!

Allow your candle to burn away safely or extinguish it with thanks. Leave the wax token to cool, then remove it and carry it with you to empower you on your path. Take the remaining seeds and the leftover apple outside and return them to the earth with thanks.

TOP TIPS FOR USING AUTUMN SPOILS

With the hedgerow at its bountiful best in September, it's hard not to run outside and gather anything and everything to eat. But you can do much more with what's out there—from beauty treatments to magical protections. Now is the perfect time to put your harvest spoils to good use!

- *Home protection.* Gather rosehips, haw berries, or rowan berries and thread them onto wire to create simple home-protection charms.

- *Ritual garlands.* Collect acorns to make garlands of thanks to the trees.

- *Wood polish.* Use oily nuts like walnuts to polish up wood. Blend the shells into a powder. Mix a spoonful of powder with water to create a cleaning paste.

- *Walking sticks.* Turn a fallen branch into a wonderful walking staff. Take it home and personalize it with stones and ribbons.

- *Bookmarks.* Collect beautiful leaves and varnish them to use as bookmarks.

- *Bird food.* Gather nuts and seeds to mix with fat in empty yogurt pots. Use these to feed the birds throughout winter.

- *Home décor.* Collect pine cones to dry ready for Yule decorations. Or make a gorgeous display from seed heads and leaves for an autumn feast.

- *Fabric dye.* Experiment with using berries to dye fabric and wool.

- *Skin treatment.* Use rosehips steeped in almond oil as an anti-aging skin treatment.

WITCHY WAYS TO CELEBRATE SEPTEMBER

- Decorate your home and altar with seed heads and berries. A bowl of brightly colored autumn leaves serves well as a focus. Burn cinnamon and sage incenses and use orange and red flowers in your decorations. A set of scales and weights can also be used to signify the time of balance.

- Work with the trees in September. Collect acorns and make simple garlands to hang in the trees as offerings.

- Cook with autumn berries and fruits. Start to make simple soups to celebrate the autumn bounty and the change in the season.

- Connect with the earth and feel part of its cycle as it starts to die back.

- Leave offerings for the spirits of the hedgerow to thank them for their bounty.

- Recognize the Goddess as the Crone, and look inward to any lessons learned. And, above all, give thanks.

- Invent new traditions to carry your magic throughout your life. Involve your family so they gain an understanding of what you believe.

- Start to preserve your food using one of the old methods, like drying or jamming.

September Folklore

"If Michaelmas brings many acorns, Christmas will cover the fields with snow."

"A dark Michaelmas, a light Christmas."

"If dry be the Buck' horn on Holy rood morn, 'tis worth a Kist of gold; but if wet it be seen, ere Holy rood e'en, bad harvest is foretold."

Chapter Eight

OCTOBER

Pumpkins all glowing orange and red

Looking like quite a funny head.

Eyes that glisten in the night

Giving us all a terrible fright!

Foods at Their Best in October

Fruits and Vegetables

apples, beetroot, black cabbage, butternut squash, curley kale, chestnuts, chard, cabbages, cardoons, celeriac, fennel, figs, kohlrabi, leeks, onions, parsnips, plums, pears, pumpkins, squashes, quinces, red kale, salsify, spinach, sweet corn, Swiss chard, swede, turnips, thyme, watercress

Seafood

brill, clams, cockle, cod, crabs, Dover sole, eel, gray mullet, haddock, hake, halibut, John Dory, lemon sole, lobster, mackerel, monkfish, mussels, plaice, scallops, squid, sea bass, skate, sea bream, oysters, turbot, winkles

Wild Foods

beech nuts, blackberry, bullace, chickweed, crab apples, duck, elderberries, giant puffball, goose, grouse, hare, hazelnut, hawthorn berries, horseradish, Jack-by-the-hedge, juniper, medlar (after the first frosts), mallard, nettles, sea aster, sloes, sea beet, sea purslane, sweet chestnut, partridge, pheasant, rowan, rosehips, teal, venison, wigeon, woodcock, wild mushrooms, wet walnuts, wood pigeon

October Correspondences

- *Festival:* Samhain (All Hallows' Eve, Halloween). Symbols include apples, pumpkins, squashes, crows, bats, ghosts, and black cats.

- *Moon name:* Hunters' Moon. Other names include Travel Moon, Blood Moon, Harvest Moon, and Dying Grass Moon.

- *Astrological signs:* Libra, September 21–October 20; Scorpio, October 21–November 20.

- *Birthstones:* Opal and tourmaline.

- *Nature spirits:* Goblins and ghouls.

- *Animals:* Cat and bats.

- *Birds:* Crow and raven.

- *Trees:* Yew.

- *Flowers:* Red roses and sedum.

- *Herbs:* Rosemary and sage.

- *Scents:* Nutmeg, cinnamon, and ginger.

- *Colors:* Black, red, and orange.

- *Goddess:* Hecate

- *Powers:* Death and rebirth; transformation and wisdom; a time when the veil between worlds is thinnest.

- *Other:* St. Francis' Day, Apple Day, Punky Night, Halloween.

In October, when the sun sits low in the sky, the beauty in the countryside is undisputed. This month heralds cool longer nights and stunning clothes for the trees. The mornings can hold that magical mist that drifts across the fields; there's a nip in the air and the evenings can be star-studded with all that twinkling up high.

But, in fact, it can be hard to find time to take a peek at Mother Nature when the clocks are set back and suddenly all is dark from dinnertime on and all you want to do is hunker down under your blanket in front of the telly. It's tempting to shut the door and lock yourself away from the early-arriving night. But if you can take a few moments each day to breathe in the October air, laced with bonfire smoke and autumnal leaves, you will feel in tune with this month. I promise! Not much seems to be going on outside, but nature is winding down to the end of the year. So make the most of even the smallest glimmer of sunshine. Who knows when we'll see it again!

October is the time of the festival of Samhain. Halloween, the Feast of the Dead—it really doesn't matter what you call it. If you head into the shops any time in October, you are treated to all manner of ghosties and ghoulies in the form of masks, costumes, even cakes! Halloween was never a big commercial celebration when I was growing up, but it has become very popular in the U.K. in the last few years. Nowadays, you cannot move for the trick-or-treaters, themed dances, and pumpkins all over Britain. We have really taken this festival to our hearts, and I say hurrah! In fact, I have a very pro-Halloween Mr. Hedgewitch at home, whose sole purpose in life at this time seems to be to watch any and every horror film there is and scare the hell out of the children.

Oh yes, many a Halloween prank has been played on my two girls. I do believe we may have scarred them for life. One year, we sent them down the pitch-black lane to the local telephone box (remember those?) with ten pence and the challenge to ring us to prove they had done it. (We knew they were perfectly safe.) And then there was the shed full of spiders, rigged on threads of cotton to fall across their faces. And the bucket of unspeakable slime, complete with fake eyeballs and a pound coin in the bottom to tempt them to reach in. And nothing gives Mr. Hedgewitch greater pleasure than making someone jump out of their skin. He is diabolically patient, too—lying in wait for a poor unsuspecting daughter just to make her jump at some perceived terror. I fear for my poor grandbabies, I really do!

On October 31, all of us who try to live the witchy way celebrate Samhain—the end of summer and the beginning of a new year. Time for some bubbly, I think! This is the ultimate festival of death and rebirth. The final harvest is in, as nature shows us in the falling leaves and the earth cooling and dying back. From now until the winter solstice, Mother Nature lies quiet, awaiting the rebirth of the sun. We honor those who have gone before us at this time—our ancestors and departed family and friends—and we pay our respects to the Fae spirits. Now is when the veil between our worlds is at its thinnest, allowing us to make contact with the other side and allowing the other side to cross and walk among us. If that scares you, remember the words my mum used to say to me: "They didn't hurt you when they were here, so they certainly won't hurt you now they've gone!" Never a truer word spoken, I think.

Divination Methods

Communication between worlds is at its best on Samhain, so any divination you perform on this night is likely to offer up a strong result. And any questions you have are more likely to be answered as well. Divination can take some practice, however, and you may have to try several methods to get answers to your questions or to look into what the future may hold for you. There are plenty of methods to choose from:

- *Scrying.* Looking into water, a crystal ball, a mirror, or flames to see and interpret shapes and signs.

- *Dowsing.* Using sticks, rods, or a pendulum to find answers to yes-or-no questions.

- *Tea leaves.* A traditional way of seeing the future by interpreting the leftover tea leaves in a cup.

- *Tarot.* Reading the pattern of the cards and the symbols to discern past, present, and future. There are many forms of tarot cards available.

- *Reading palms.* Following the lines on the hand to foretell life events.

- *Runes.* Interpreting symbols painted or engraved on sets of stones or wood.

- *Automatic writing.* Writing without thinking, usually done in a meditative state.

These are just a few divination methods you can try; this is by no means an exhaustive list. One technique may suit you better than the others. This is definitely the right time of year to have a go and pick up a new skill.

Samhain Ritual

You will need:

A candle

A small sprig of rosemary, or a pinch of dried plant

A sage leaf, or a pinch of dried plant

Sit somewhere quiet and dark. Take a few slow, deep breaths to focus. When you are ready, light the candle and place it in front of you. Hold the rosemary in your hand and connect with its remembrance properties.

Look into the flame of the candle and visualize a loved one or ancestor sitting on the other side of the candle. When you are ready, burn the rosemary in the candle flame and say:

I will remember and hold you dear,
I send you blessings this coming year.

Then take the sage in your hand and connect with its wisdom properties. Look into the flame of the candle and visualize it passing you wisdom through its dancing flame. When you are ready, burn the sage in the candle flame and say:

Wisdom from the other world,
Messages now start to unfurl.

Continue to watch the flame of the candle dance. Be aware of anything that is shown to you in the shapes of the flame or in your mind's eye. When you have received the wisdom you seek, allow the candle to burn down safely with thanks and record your experience in your Book of Shadows.

This simple ritual is great for honing your divination skills. Practice it as often as you can and see what you are shown.

Honoring the Past

Some of the traditional ways of Samhain are still as relevant today as they were for our ancestors. Lighting candles in front of old pictures of our loved ones and setting a place at the table for dinner are still wonderful ways to honor those who have gone before us. I know your family will look at you as if you have gone completely mad when you start to dish up a portion for an invisible diner, but think of it as an amazing conversation-starter. Talking about your ancestors is the ultimate way to honor them!

You keep someone very much alive in the tales you tell and the stories you remember. Family will draw close to you to listen and remember with you, and will share in your laughter and tears. Toast your loved ones with a glass of wine, light candles and incense in their name, carry something they owned with you, and make them part of your celebration on this night. And don't forget to honor the animals that have passed on as well. Some milk in a bowl or some biscuits at the table are wonderful ways to remember our beloved pets.

Once you have finished your meal, don't clear away the plate set for your ancestor. Leave it until the following day if you can. Remember, the food may still be there the next day, but the essence of it will have been consumed. And be sure to leave some food out for the spirits of the Fae. Put a little treat out on the doorstep for the faeries that may come past, and put some out in your home for the faeries that live with you. The Fae folk are especially mischievous at Samhain, so best we keep them happy!

How do you know whether or not you have been joined by spirits from the other side? It may be something as simple as the hairs standing up on your arms, or a familiar smell, or a faint breeze. Be watchful for the signs and always remember to thank the spirits for their presence at the end of your Samhain meal. They have helped shape you into what you are today. Although we remember our ancestors at Samhain, we don't have to be all morbid and serious about it. Samhain is a great excuse for a party—as if we needed an excuse!

Of all the traditions we honor at this time of year, the one that seems to be growing in popularity is trick-or-treating. In Britain, this tradition used to be observed on All Souls' Day, when the poor went door to door begging for food. They were given small cakes called "soul cakes" on the promise that they would say a prayer for the dead. Ghostly carved-out pumpkins, or jack-o'-lanterns, were originally made from turnips. The story was that Jack tried to outwit the devil by getting him to agree never to take his soul. When Jack died, however, he wasn't virtuous enough to go to heaven, so he was sentenced to walk the earth forever. He complained about how dark it was, so the devil tossed him a piece of hot coal, which Jack placed in a hollowed-out turnip so he could carry it around to guide him.

Apple bobbing is another tradition we observe at home on Samhain. Although its true origins are not known, it has always been thought to be a means of divination. When an apple is caught, its skin is peeled in one long strip. The peel is then dropped to the floor and its shape is said to give the initial of your true love.

Black Cats—Unlucky?

One of the symbols for Samhain, and for the more commercial festival of Halloween, is the beautiful black cat. So much folklore and legend surrounds our dark-haired feline friends that it has given rise over the years to unspeakable things being done to them at this time of year. This makes me so incredibly sad and worried—not least for my own black fur babies when they are out and about on their travels.

Most of the folklore about black cats portrays them as the archetype of the witch's familiar, and therefore as unlucky. In the U.K., when a black cat crosses your path, it is considered lucky. In the United States, it is considered a sign of imminent evil. Walking under a ladder after a black cat is said to bring you double bad luck; but petting a black cat's tail is thought to cure a sty in the eye. Meeting a black cat at midnight is to meet the devil himself; but to dream of a black cat is to foretell good fortune!

To me, black cats are just the same as any other cat—maybe with just a hint more mystery about them. I consider myself very lucky to have three black cats in my life. One of them is the daughter of my original two babies, who have an interesting history. Here is their story.

Mr. Hedgewitch has always been a dog person. Even the fiercest of dogs roll over for a tummy tickle when he approaches. I, however, have always been a crazy cat lady. After much pleading and big sad eyes, he relented and said we could get a cat. Hurrah! So, with my heart set on a little male furry friend, we located a kitten not far from us and off we tripped to bring him home. He was a very timid little thing, scared of the dogs and the general household noise. I named him Samhain, because it was that time of year, and I comforted him as much as I could. It was during this comforting that I discovered that my dear little boy was, in fact, a girl! How did I miss that? We changed her name to Meg.

Well, we decided, after a lot of discussion, that this little one really needed a friend, someone to play with and bring her out of herself. So we set off to collect another fur baby—a beautiful black fluffy kitten full of confidence and cheek. We named him Frank, and Frank really did bring Meg out of her shell A couple of days later, we took Meg and Frank down to the local vet for their checkups and vaccinations. The vet declared Meg to be a healthy girl, and then declared Frank to be healthy, but definitely not a boy. I couldn't believe I had made the same mistake again, although the vet said it was very common. So now I had two girls when I had set out to have one boy!

In retrospect, I think there must have been a reason why I ended up with these two. I think I was meant to have them. Frank's name was swiftly changed to Frankie, and she and Meg both settled in well. Meg soon became Peg, then Peggles, my beloved familiar. Frankie became Frankiedoodle, and then just Doodle. Peggles and Doodle are still with us today, and are so very loved. Wookie, the daughter of Doodle, is our other black girl, and the latest addition to the clan is Merlin, a handsome black-and-white *boy*. Oh yes, I checked properly this time!

Samhain Loaf Cake

This easy, moist loaf cake is a great way to use up the insides of all those pumpkins that get carved for your celebrations. Yes, they're good for more than soup! This is a lovely cake to offer everyone at the end of your Samhain ritual or meal.

Ingredients

600 g./21 oz. pumpkin, peeled, seeds removed, and cubed

1 tbsp. oil

100 g./3.5 oz. unsalted butter

300 g./10.5 oz. soft light brown sugar

2 eggs

500 g./17.5 oz. self-rising flour

½ tsp. baking soda

1 tsp. ground cinnamon

½ tsp. each ground ginger, cloves, and nutmeg

2 small or one large eating apple, cored and chopped

Method

1. Preheat the oven to 100°C/200°F.

2. Grease and line a 900 g./32 oz. loaf tin with waxed paper.

3. Place the pumpkin in a roasting tray and drizzle with the oil. Cover with foil and roast for 25 minutes.

4. Remove from the roasting tray and set aside to cool. Blend the pumpkin in a food processor until smooth.

5. Increase the oven to 180°C/350°F.

6. Cream the butter and sugar in a mixing bowl until light and fluffy. Add the eggs and pumpkin, and stir until well combined.

7. Stir in all the dry ingredients and the chopped apple. Place the mixture in the loaf tin and smooth the top. You can sprinkle the top with some of the pumpkin seeds you removed.

1. Bake for 50 minutes. Remove the tin from the oven. Once cool, remove the loaf from the tin to a cooling rack.

1. Sprinkle with icing sugar and cinnamon to serve.

The Moon

The moon has fascinated us here on earth for all of time. That wonderful, amazing, heavenly body that seems to be floating above us mirrors who we are. As a feminine energy, the moon changes in the way our seasons and cycles change—waxing and waning, controlling our tides and time, regulating our menstrual patterns, and influencing our behavior. Because the moon is a celestial body that lends powerful energies to our magical work, it is very important that we understand its cycles and what magic will work best during each of its phases.

The monthly celebration of the moon is called an Esbat. These can be performed on the new moon or, more commonly, on the full moon. An Esbat allows you to draw down the power of the moon, hold it inside you, and channel it into any healing or spell work. Once you have completed your work, you can convey the moon's power down into Mother Earth. Esbats are a wonderful time for personal development. Who can fail to be enchanted by the silvery force of the moon on a clear night? I find some guides to working with the moon to be a little complicated. So here's what I use as a reference for my magic:

- *Waxing moon.* Crescent is on the right. Spells for new beginnings, abundance, luck, love, and health. A time to sow seeds.

- *Full moon.* Moon is round in the sky. Spells for positivity, knowledge, healing, and success. The strongest time for lunar energy; a time to charge things.

- *Waning moon.* Crescent is on the left. Spells for banishing, habit-breaking, and mood.

- *New moon.* Dark moon, no longer visible. Spells for rest and inner work.

Magic worked with the help of Lady Moon can be fine-tuned by taking into account the astrological sign of the full moon. Now I know this can get a little confusing, and I freely admit that it's not always something I do in my own moon magic. But it can be useful to know the moon's power in each star sign.

Moon in Aries: Spells for leadership and power; healing for the face and head.

Moon in Taurus: Spells for love and money; healing for the throat and ears.

Moon in Gemini: Spells for communication and travel; healing for the shoulders and arms.

Moon in Cancer: Spells for the home and hearth; healing for the chest and stomach.

Moon in Leo: Spells for courage and fertility; healing for the spine and heart.

Moon in Virgo: Spells for intelligence and work; healing for the intestines and nervous system.

Moon in Libra: Spells for unions and balance; healing for the back and kidneys.

Moon in Scorpio: Spells for sex and growth; healing for the reproductive system.

Moon in Sagittarius: Spells for travel and justice; healing for the liver and upper legs.

Moon in Capricorn: Spells for career and drive; healing for all bones and teeth.

Moon in Aquarius: Spells for freedom and friendship; healing for lower legs and blood.

Moon in Pisces: Spells for dreams and creativity; healing for feet and glands.

The star signs for each month can be found at the beginning of each chapter, so you can cross-reference the star sign in which the full moon appears each month.

The moon can have a very powerful influence on our magical workings, so spelling for the right thing at the right time will make your magic more successful. Makes sense, right? Well, that is generally the case, but you have to use your own judgment here and be wise. If you need to spell for healing, for example, waiting for the right phase of the moon is probably not going to help! Some things just can't wait. So follow your heart and work in a way that's best for you at the time. It is definitely worth making a note of the moon phases in your Book of Shadows and seeing what energy the moon lends to your magic. You will soon start to see a pattern of what's working well and when.

Moon Water

Each month on the full moon, I make my moon water. With the moon lending her highest energy at that time, I like to charge water for magical use throughout the month. It carries the lunar energy and can add a big pinch of power to simple spells. Here's how I make it.

Take a clear glass bowl and fill it with pure water. You can use rain water, spring water, or tap water. Drop a clear quartz crystal or a moonstone into the bowl. (This is optional, but it does add a bit of extra power.)

After the sun has set, take the bowl outside to sit in the rays of the full moon. It doesn't have to be a clear night for this to work. The moon's energy will penetrate the clouds. Hold your hands on either side of the bowl and say:

Mother moon, strong and bright, charge this water for me tonight.

Drape a piece of fine muslin over the bowl to stop any wandering bugs from getting into the water. Leave the bowl out overnight to absorb the powerful moon rays.

Get up before the sun rises if you can. Otherwise, as soon as you do get up, go and retrieve the moon water. Decant it into a bottle to be used for magic for the coming month. Give any moon water remaining at the end of the month to your plants as an offering.

Moon water can be used in all sorts of ways. For a magical bath, add a few drops to your bath water. Add some to meals you are making. Use it to wash your hands before magical work, or dot it on your third eye before divination or meditation. Add some to your pet's drinking water for gentle healing, or use it as an offering to the plants and trees.

Sloe Gin (approx. 70 cl./24.5 oz.)

The fruit of the magical blackthorn is by far my favorite target for foraging—because I love sloe gin! Hopefully, by October, the first frosts have come and gone, softening the sloes' skin a little. But if it's been a fairly mild October, a night in the freezer will do the job for you just as well.

Ingredients

450 g./16 oz. sloes, washed

350 g./12.5 oz. white sugar

70 cl./24.5 oz bottle of gin, plus an empty bottle

of the same size

Method

1. Prick the sloes with a fork to make a few holes.

2. Divide the sloes, sugar, and gin between the two bottles and seal. Shake well.

3. Leave somewhere cool and dark for around 3 months, shaking occasionally.

4. Your sloe gin should be ready for you to toast Yule!

Sloe Gin Jelly

Ingredients

350 ml./12 oz. sloe gin

150 ml./5 oz. water

100 g./3.5 oz. sugar

8 leaves of gelatine (or 1 ¼ envelopes of

    U.S. powdered gelatine) plus a small amount

    of cold water to soak it in.

Method

1. If using gelatine leaves, soak the gelatine in a little cold water to soften it.

2. Bring the sugar and water to a boil. Use some of your moon water for this to lend your jelly extra power.

3. Remove the soaked gelatine from the cold water and dissolve it in the sugar and water. If using powdered gelatine, sprinkle it into the dissolved sugar water solution now.

4. Once the gelatine has dissolved, remove the pan from the heat and allow it to cool for a couple of minutes.

5. Pour the sloe gin into the syrup, stir to combine well, and pour into a mould.

6. Place in the fridge and leave to set for at least 4 hours.

7. Serve with cream—for adults only!

Children and Magic

If you don't have children around, then you have my apologies and can skip the next section. But for all of us who *do* have little darlings around—our own, or grandchildren, or nieces, or nephews, or children of friends that just appear out of nowhere—this is for you.

There are upsides and downsides to working with children magically. On the upside, children are the most magical beings on the earth! They seem to be born with an inherent ability to see into the world of Fae, and can pick up on energies from the time they are born. Young children are completely beguiled by characters like Harry Potter and places like Hogwarts, and they can find magic in the most mundane things. On the downside, they do have the attention span of gnats and rarely accept anything you say without asking "Why?" Older children can be more difficult still—with their "street cred" apparently being of utmost importance. Well, let's just say that unless it involves a sparkly vampire, they won't even raise their heads!

So how do you even begin to involve your children in your magical world? Well, if you can grab them when they're young, it is certainly less tricky. But there are ways in which all children can start to practice magic, whatever their age. Here are some ideas that you can try with your little witchy ones:

- *Water.* Kids love water! Oh yes, you may get drenched, but keeping their interest while having fun is what it's all about. If you have a river near or you live by the sea, have your child draw a picture or write a wish and cast it into the water. Or tie the paper to a stick and play Pooh sticks off a bridge. If you don't have access to natural water, use a paddling pool or even a bowl of water. Show your child how to make ripples on the water to send out wishes, or drop stones in to make a splash so the faeries can have a shower! Magical baths work well with kids, too. Add bubbles and flowers, and play swirling games in the bath to release the healing powers of the plants.

- *Air.* Kites, balloons, and bubbles can all be used to carry wishes and dreams, or worries and concerns, away. Tie a leaf to a balloon and release it to the air to say thanks to the trees. Blowing bubbles never gets old for me. See how far the bubbles can go without bursting, and imagine that the rainbow colors are

Faerie clothes. Stand on a hill and shout your worries to the wind to be carried away.

- *Fire.* Never unsupervised! If you're in a safe place with full supervision, candle magic is great for children. Get them to carve a picture of a favorite animal or person on a candle with a toothpick, then burn the candle. A smallcamp fire is a wonderful place to tell old tales and try out divination techniques by watching the flames.

- *Earth.* Children love to dig! A small trowel and a patch of earth or sand will soon result in a hole. Once dug, ask your child to place stones in the hole to represent anything they wish to leave behind—any nightmares or bad feelings they want to bury. Rocks can be painted to give a focus when a child is unhappy and crystals can be made into a relaxing crystal garden for his or her room.

- *Goddess and God.* Go for a walk and talk about everything you see. Does the child think the things you see represent male or female energy? Look for the Green Man in the trees and the Goddess in the flowers. Make moon water and sun water together.

- *Plants.* Children love to watch things grow, so sow some seeds. Plant bulbs and give the child the responsibility of looking after them. Encourage children to talk to their plants and to handle them gently. Show them how to nourish the plant with food and water.

- *Faery houses.* Children love to look for faeries and goblins. Build a small shelter for them out of sticks. Leave food out for the Fae as an offering. While you're building with sticks, find a nice one to take home as a wand.

- *Birds.* Encourage your children to scatter seed for the birds and forage in the hedgerow for wild food that they eat. Collect feathers to make a picture to remind them of their responsibility to feed the birds—or any other animal, for that matter!

- *Dance.* Put on some music and get your groove on! Leap and hop around; encourage your children to pretend to be all different sorts of animals to help them connect with wildlife.

- *Cook.* I have yet to meet a child who doesn't like the magic of cookery. Measure and stir, talk about where the ingredients come from, and look in wonder at the way cooking transforms food.

- *Laugh.* Laughter is the sound of how we want the world to be, so laugh long and hard every day.

CHILDREN AND THE WHEEL OF THE YEAR

Children love "special" days. So, if you can, start a calendar of the Wheel of the Year. On each day, write down an activity that you can do together to mark that day—sort of like a birthday for Mother Nature, only more than once a year. All kids know when their birthdays are and that they'll get presents and cakes to celebrate that special day. My two girls placed huge importance on their birthdays every year. Honestly, you would think they were actual princesses!

You don't have to do big things to celebrate the turning of the Wheel—maybe just a picnic at summer solstice or finding and decorating a Yule log at Yule. Use a bulletin board in the bedroom of an older child to pin symbols of the seasons to special days. Autumn leaves and dried flowers work well, but magazine cuttings are useful here too. Take the board down every festival and renew it together. If all else fails, try face painting! Children love to become something else. Not the teenagers, though! It's a brave parent who tries to paint over a teenage girl's makeup in the name of magic!

Let your children have a go at painting your face, too. When was the last time you were turned into a bumble bee or a butterfly? To connect a child to magic, you first have to connect to your own child within. Sounds a bit hippy, but it is so true.

Have a theme for the year—maybe trees one year, flowers the next, etc. Make each festival fun and your child will look forward to them in the same way you do. Make this an opportunity to encourage them to give thanks for the turning of the Wheel. Now, where on earth did I put those face wipes to get this stuff off my face?

THE BATHROOM CABINET

After removing the face paint and sticky residue left over from all the magic with the children, it's time to see what else you have lurking in the back of your bathroom cabinet. If it's like mine, you will have lots of shampoo. I always buy it when I buy conditioner, but I always run out of conditioner before shampoo, leaving me with too many bottles! There will probably be some shaving cream (Mr. Hedgewitch's, not mine, I hasten to add), toothpaste, and some nondescript soap that you rarely use.

With all these unassuming things lurking in the cabinet, I think it's time we put them to good use. So here are a few ways to use up some of that leftover bathroom stuff. Now that's what I call recycling!

Toothpaste

A blob of toothpaste can:

Stop the itching of an insect bite

Dry out a blemish

Clean your nails—after all, our nails are made from the same stuff as our teeth

Deodorize smelly garlic or onion hands

Remove stains from carpets, shoes, and walls

Polish up your silver jewelry

Shampoo

A squeeze of shampoo can:

Lubricate door hinges, and tighten nuts and bolts

Gently clean leather

Clean your car

Wash your underwear—a great one for when you're on holiday

Make great shaving foam

Soap

A bar of soap can:

Keep your drawers moving freely—just rub some along the runners

Make needles and pins glide through fabric with ease

Loosen a stuck zipper

Keep the bugs off your plants—just mix it with water and wipe the leaves

Keep your clothes smelling fresh—just pop a bar into your drawers

Shaving Foam

A dollop of shaving foam can:

Clean your hands

Stop your mirror from steaming up—just wipe on before you hit the shower

Decorate your windows at Yule time

Clean and deodorize any pet mishaps

Degrease your oven—just spray, leave, then rinse

Witchy Ways to Celebrate October

- Decorate your home and altar with all things Samhain! Use pumpkins, squashes, and apples as your focus, and light red, black, and orange candles. Burn nutmeg and cinnamon incense, or sage for wisdom.

- Work with the children if you can, and celebrate the old Samhain traditions.

- Cook a favorite meal for a departed loved one and gather the family to talk about that person or pet.

- Try divination and record your results in your Book of Shadows.

- Connect with your ancestors; meditate on how they lived and what this time of year meant for them.

- Celebrate the death and rebirth of the earth by tying up loose ends and starting anew.

October Folklore

"Rain in October means wind in December."

"When berries are many in October, beware a hard winter."

"If the October moon comes with no frost, expect no frost till the moon of November."

"In October, dig your fields, and your land its wealth shall yield!"

Chapter Nine

NOVEMBER

Crows fly high in the cold month sky
Flapping around like rags on high.
The land is sleeping with no more mirth
Awaiting the return of the cosmic birth.

Foods at Their Best in November

Fruits and Vegetables

butternut squash, brussels sprouts, beetroot, clementines, chicory, cabbages, celeriac, celery, chard, cranberries, Jerusalem artichokes, kale, kohlrabi, leeks, onions, pears, pumpkins, pomegranate, parsnips, quince, salsify, satsumas, swede, Swiss chard, turnips, tangerines

Seafood

brill, clams, crab, Dover sole, eel, halibut, hake, haddock, John Dory, langoustine, lemon sole, lobster, monkfish, mussels, oysters, pollack, plaice, skate, scallops, squid, sea bass, turbot, winkles

Wild Foods

chestnuts, chickweed, duck, goose, grouse, guinea fowl, hare, horseradish, mallard, medlars, hazelnut, nettles, pheasant, partridges, rosehips, teal, sea beet, sea purslane, venison, wild mushrooms, wild rabbit, woodcock, wigeon, wood pigeon, walnuts

November Correspondences

- *Festival*: All Hallows' Day.

- *Moon name*: Beaver Moon. Other names include Frost Moon, Snow Moon, and Hunters' Moon.

- *Astrological signs*: Scorpio, October 21–November 20; Sagittarius, November 21–December 20.

- *Birthstones*: Topaz and citrine.

- *Nature spirits*: Banshees and underworld spirits.

- *Animals*: Sow and wolf.

- *Birds*: Rooks and magpies.

- *Trees*: Blackthorn.

- *Flowers*: Lilies and orchids.

- *Herbs*: Wormwood and thyme.

- *Scents*: Nutmeg and rosemary.

- *Colors*: White and deep purple.

- *Goddess*: Cerridwen.

- *Powers*: New beginnings and endings; letting go.

- *Other*: All Saints' Day, All Souls' Day, Mischief Night, Bonfire Night, Armistice Day (Martinmas), St. Andrew's Day (Scotland).

You can tell it's November by that certain smell of winter approaching. The nights start at 4:00 in the afternoon and seem to roll on endlessly. It's harder to get up in the morning (as if it were ever easy), as the darkness shortens the daylight hours. Oh yes, there is no mistaking this month—if only because of the sheer panic of realizing that Christmas is round the corner. Only one monthly payday left and you haven't even started to prepare! So now is the time, probably more than any other month, when we want to stay inside and draw the curtains, put on the lights, and veg out at home. After all, who wants to go traipsing around in the cold and dark?

In the U.K., there is one exception to this "hiding out" at home. On November 5, we all bundle up in our coats and fight our way through the darkness to stand by a bonfire topped with the effigy of a man, eat hotdogs, and watch displays of fireworks light up the winter sky. Bonfire night, or Guy Fawkes Night, is a tradition that is still popular today. It celebrates the day in 1605 when a plot to blow up King James I failed. Back then, bonfires were lit around London to celebrate the failure of the plot. Soon after, November 5 was declared a day of public thanksgiving.

Have you fallen asleep with all this history? Me too. So back to the day's celebrations. I have stood in the pouring rain, faced howling winds, and shivered through freezing temperatures to watch ten minutes of pretty lights in the sky with the children—who, as it turned out, were never that interested anyway. I will share with you one particularly bad night many years ago, when we had tickets to the local bonfire event. It was very, very wet and windy, so we drove to my Uncle Jim's to park the car closer to the festivities so we wouldn't have far to walk. After a sweet sherry (bless him) and a quick chat, we headed off to the local football field to watch the fireworks and get drenched.

When the event was over, we herded the bedraggled children back to the car. I decided that, rather than disturb my poor elderly uncle again, we would just quietly get in the car and head home. I didn't think any more about it, until I had a phone call from Uncle Jim a few days later, checking to see if we were all okay. Shouting down the phone (he was more than a little deaf), he said he had been worried about us when he realized the car was gone. But, even worse, he had heated up soup and laid the table ready for our return from the rain. I was completely mortified. I don't think anything has ever made me cringe with embarrassment more. I felt so bad! Uncle Jim forgave me, of course, but I have never forgotten that night and neither have my darling girls, who love to taunt me with the tale of when poor Uncle Jim sat there with a saucepan of soup with no one to eat it. Wow, even now I can feel myself cringing.

So, tip for this month: If you have an elderly uncle, always make sure you say goodbye before you leave. It'll haunt you for the rest of your days if you don't!

Bonfire Freeform Pie

I love to make this recipe for bonfire night. It's easy to throw together, looks great, and smells wonderful with all the baked onions. Prebake your onions the day before if you can to allow them to cool completely before you make your pie. Then just add ketchup for dipping.

Ingredients for the crust

400 g./14 oz. strong white flour

1 tsp. chili powder

5 tsp. smoked sweet paprika

2 tsp. salt

½ tsp. baking powder

50 g./1.5 oz. unsalted butter

25 ml./1 oz. olive oil

1 medium egg

About 100 ml./3.5 oz. water

Ingredients for the filling

A couple of potatoes, cooked in their skins

100–200 g./3.5–7 oz. sliced ham

8–10 roasted medium onions

2 tbsp. chopped fresh thyme or 1 tbsp. of dried herb

Beaten egg to glaze

Salt and pepper

Method

1. Wash and bake the onions in their skins in a medium oven until they collapse, then cool and peel.

2. To make the pastry, put the flour, spices, salt, and baking powder in a bowl. Add the butter and oil, and rub everything together with your fingers.

3. Add the egg and most of the water, and work into a smooth dough, adding more water if it's a little dry. Wrap up the dough and leave it to rest for about an hour in the fridge.

4. Line a baking tray with waxed paper and heat the oven to 200°C/400°F.

5. Roll half the dough into a rectangle .5 cm./.25 inch thick and lay this on the tray. Slice the potatoes, skin on, and lay them across the dough, leaving a 2 cm./.75 inch border.

6. Sprinkle on half the thyme and season well. Next, lay the ham and onions over the potatoes. Top with the rest of the thyme and season again.

7. Roll the remaining dough out to the same size as the first and lay this over the filling. Twist the edges up and together to make a neat border, brush with beaten egg, and slash across the top.

8. Bake for about 40 minutes, until the filling is sizzling inside and the crust is a rich, golden brown.

You can ring the changes with this rustic pie. Just remove the ham and add grated cheese and butternut squash for a great veggie alternative. Serve with potato wedges and seasonal vegetables, or eat cold with a simple beetroot salad.

Your Magical Home

Bonfire night aside, it seems, on the face of it, that there is very little to celebrate in November. But this gives us a perfect opportunity to look to the place where we spend most of our time—in our homes. If you are like me, you see your home as a magical sanctuary that oozes charm, character, and mystery. In reality, it is probably a space that is overtaken by your partner's shoes (I really wish he would move them), crowded with your children's toys, marred by your pet's muddy paw prints, and covered with a layer of dust that you always insist will never get any deeper!

Tackling the realities of your home environment and starting to turn it into the image you have in your head is no mean feat. You always end up having to make compromises. But you can make a real difference if you are a little bit sneaky about it. And, let's face it, no one else in the house will probably even notice anything's different!

Your magical home should always start at your front door. After all, it's the first place you see when you get home and it is the magical threshold into your living space. For Hedgewitches, any threshold is a magical place. So I think it is important to spend some time blessing and protecting the one we use the most. The doorstep, the door frame, and the door itself all hold threshold energy and reflect what's hidden behind them. So much folklore surrounds the entrances to houses that it would take a whole book to cover it—and there probably is one out there somewhere!

It requires a little lateral thinking to make the inside of your home a more magical space. If you live on your own, it is relatively easy to invoke a feeling of magic, because you only have yourself to please. But if you have others living in the space, it becomes so much harder. It can be tempting, especially if you are just starting out on your path, to fill your home with so much magical equipment that it looks like a witches' shop. At that point, even the most understanding of partners and the most placid children (if there are such beings) can start tutting and moaning in a way that can undermine all the positivity you want to create.

You don't need everything to be from a specialist shop to make your home magical. Just some normal household items will do the same job. It's the intent that you put into these things that help make your home magical. Think about touching all your senses in each room and you won't go far wrong. Here are a few ideas to help you create your magical home.

The Threshold

I think that a good place to start to make your threshold magical is to clean it. I know this sounds a bit obvious, but how many of us clean our front door regularly? Make the cleaning of your front door a ritual—a cleansing task that can be imbued with positivity. Use hot water mixed with lemon or rosemary for cleansing and wash the whole area in a clockwise (deosil) motion.

As you wash, imagine the area being cleansed, not only of any grime, but also of any negativity that may have touched it. Wash away all those bad days at work or arguments that have transferred via the door handle. You can say some simple words, like:

Threshold of mine be cleansed today,
All negativity I now wash away.

Once you've cleansed your threshold, it is ready to be blessed and protected. I find the simplest way of doing this is to draw a magical symbol on it. You can use any oil for this, although olive oil is particularly effective. Dip your finger into the oil and draw a symbol that represents protection to you on the door, its frame, and the doorstep. It may be a simple flame, a star, a pentacle—anything that means protection to you. As you do this, say some simple words to seal your protection, like:

I ask for blessings, three times three
May they be granted, so mote it be!

If you don't want to use oil, you can use water, or maybe even clear nail varnish for a more permanent symbol. Waft incense over the area, or sprinkle blessed water, or simply light a candle.

Once your threshold has been cleansed and blessed, call for protection. There are lots of ways to protect your front door—from hanging wreaths on it to adorning it with strings of garlic. I like to place a simple pot of sage at the front door and put two crossed needles under the door mat. If you have soft-pawed pets that use the entrance, however, use knitting needles crossed under the mat, because sewing needles can be a hazard for them. Place some sage leaves on top of the porch or bury a small packet of dill seeds next to the door. Burying jasmine at the corners outside the house works well, too. Remember to charge your protection objects before you place them.

The Living Room

As a place where we all tend to congregate these days, the living room has taken over from the kitchen as the heart of the home. In our house, this is where we shout at the TV (hopefully not at each other) and fight for sofa space with the wealth of dogs and cats. Making your living room more magical can easily be achieved by deploying subtle witchy ways around the room. Here are everyday items you can use that you probably have around the house already:

- *Crystals.* Hang a simple crystal in the window to cast bouncing rainbows of light to bless the walls.

- *Candles.* Light a small candle every day to bless all those who enter.

- *Salt.* Place a small packet of salt to absorb any negativity from the inevitable disagreements that take place in any home.

- *Herbs.* Hide a sachet of comforting herbs in the cushion covers.

- *Incense.* Light incense for fragrance and lift it to bless the four corners of the room.

- *Flowers.* Arrange fresh flowers to bring life into the area.

- *Décor.* Redecorate your room on the new moon to bring in luck.

- *Furniture.* Use rounded-off furniture or rugs instead of sharp-cornered items to increase the circulation of energy.

- *Pictures.* Hang a pretty picture of flowers or trees, or grow potted plants to bring their essence into the space and give you a focus for meditation.

The Kitchen

The kitchen is the ultimate area for magical workings. It is the room where the alchemy of food takes place daily and where, at least in my house, the kettle gets put on more times in a day than I care to mention. Remember, anything you create, from a cuppa to a three-course meal, is an offering of thanks served up on the kitchen table.

Making the kitchen and the things in it magical can be as simple or as complicated as you like. Cupboards can hold a wealth of secrets stashed at the back. But for a more general magical kitchen, here are a few ideas:

- *Herbs.* Fill pretty jars with herbs for cooking and spell work.

- *Garlic.* Put a bulb of garlic on the windowsill to protect the space. Remember never to eat it, however.

- *Equipment.* Bless all your kitchen appliances, dishwasher to fridge, with a magical symbol to empower them to help you in your workings.

- *Oven.* Keep a clean oven. Your oven takes the place of the old hearth fire, so remove any residue from it daily by wiping it out and saying a simple blessing of thanks.

- *Candles.* Light a small candle whenever you cook to invoke the fire element to help you.

- *Tea.* Keep a small teapot, a cup, and a saucer on the side for your magical teas.

- *Fruit.* Bless a display of fruit in a bowl for the good health of the family.

- *Cupboards.* Place protection-and-abundance herbs on top of your kitchen cupboards, and remember to change them regularly.

The Bedroom

This is the room where we spend so much time, although it sometimes feels as if we are never in it. The bedroom can be arranged magically to help you get a good night's sleep, to bring you wonderful dreams, and perhaps even to encourage a hint of passion once in a while! A comfortable bed and soft colors can help this room become a sanctuary. But here are a few other ways you can magically empower your bedroom to help you get through your day-to-day life:

- *Altar.* Create a mini-altar on top of your chest of drawers that symbolizes what you want from your bedroom. Use fabric or pretty scarves to drape across the top.

- *Crystals.* Arrange a few crystals in a tray of sand to create a wonderful focus of peace for the room.

- *Sachets.* Tuck a small sachet of lavender and oats under your pillow to encourage peaceful sleep.

- *Holly.* Place holly under the bed to stop nightmares.

- *Oils.* Wipe your bedroom light bulbs with essential oil of lavender or rose to spread a wonderful fragrance through the room.

- *Water.* Have a special glass filled with water next to your bed, charged with purifying you to make you ready for sleep.

- *Dreams.* Keep a notebook and pen next to your bed to write down your dreams.

- *Flowers.* Keep fresh flowers or small branches of foliage in a red vase for passion and love.

- *Bell.* Keep a small bell by your bed to ring as you retire. This can chase away negative thoughts.

The Bathroom

This is the room of cleansing. Moreover, the bathroom is probably the only private room in your home with a lock on the door. Whether you're a shower person or a soak-in-the-tub person, the bathroom offers a wonderful space to bring magic into your home. Here are some everyday items you can use:

- *Shells.* Use shells and driftwood to symbolize the element of water.

- *Candles.* Place small candles in pretty soap dishes and light them (safely) to bring a magical atmosphere.

- *Motto*. Hang a simple quote in a frame to use as a focus while you bathe; make it a positive one!

- *Oils*. Put bottles of magical oils along the windowsill to absorb the power of the sun and moon. Dot the inside of the toilet roll tube with essential oil to release its fragrance when the roll is used.

- *Bath blessings*. Keep squares of muslin in your bathroom cabinet with ribbons to create bath blessings.

- *Soap*. Inscribe magical symbols in a new bar of soap to bless all who use it.

- *Salt*. Keep a small container of salt handy and add a few grains to your bathwater for ritual cleansing, or to cleanse the water before it goes down the drain.

Magical Baths

This seems like a good place to stop and take a look at magical baths. Bathing is something we all do every day—or at least I hope we do! Whether you hit the shower or wallow with a good book, the time you take to cleanse yourself is a wonderful ritual that can be transformed into spell work.

I myself am a wallow-for-ages kind of girl—even more so now that the children have grown up and flown away. No more chubby little fingers creeping under the bathroom door; no more pleading voices whining, "I really need to go." My hard-earned bathroom bliss has finally arrived. Hurrah! To all of you whose bathroom time is still being invaded, you have my deepest sympathies. I promise you it will end one day and you will be able to reclaim your bathroom rights. By the way, this invasion of bathroom time is by no means limited to children. My friend Karen has yet to claim a private shower without the company of her cat, Amber!

Creating a magical bath can be a really simple way to connect with all the elements—steam for air, candles for fire, bath salts for earth, and water for, well, water! No one, however, can be completely immersed in a magical bathing experience when there's a ring round the tub or the dreaded hair in the drain. Before you start to use your bath time as a time for spell work, make sure everything is squeaky clean. After all, all that grime carries the energy of things shed off by yourself and others, and combining the discarded with the new is never good when working magic.

There are several ways in which you can use the bath or shower to work your spells. Most involve the use of herbs or plants in one way or another. Creating simple bath blessings using herbs tied up in a square of muslin is a wonderful way to empower your spell and then bathe in its magical energy.

Bath Blessings

To make a bath blessing, gather all the ingredients you wish to put into your spell. Sit somewhere quiet and light a candle. If you are doing this in the bathroom, which I think is the best place, light a few candles and work solely by candlelight.

In a small bowl, mix together your blessing ingredients so their energies blend. Place the mixture into the center of a square of muslin, draw up the corners, and tie with the appropriate color ribbon, or with a universal white thread.

While your bath is running, hold your bath blessing in your hand and close your eyes. Focus on what you want from the blessing, and imagine your energy flowing to mix with the other ingredients. You can say a few simple words over and over, like these:

Energy flows from me to thee,
Empowering my spell, so mote it be!

Drop the bath blessing into the water to swirl as the bath continues to run. Focus on the water becoming magically charged with the ingredients of your spell. When the bath has run, step into it and submerge yourself in the magical water. Swirl the water around you, focusing on the spell enveloping you, becoming part of you and you of it.

Close your eyes and breathe in the steam, inhaling the spell you have created. Spend time absorbing the power of your spell. When you are ready, step out of the bath and remove the blessing. Sprinkle a few grains of salt into the water to cleanse it of any negativity before it leaves your home.

Bath blessings can be as simple or as complicated as you like. I tend to use two bases—milk powder or oats—and one or two herbs at the most. You can also use essential oils in your bath blessings; just a few drops will do. Here are a few combinations that I regularly mix with milk powder or oats for my spell work:

Lavender: peace

Blossom petals: gentle world healing

Rosemary and lemon zest: cleansing

Rose petals: love

Bay: wish fulfillment

Thyme: healing

Sage: wisdom

Basil: passion

Cinnamon: money

Creating a bath blessing will work if you're a shower person too. Just make the ribbon a bit longer and allow the shower water to run over the blessing, infusing your shower and the steam with its power.

Bath blessings are only one way to have magical bathing time. There are so many other ways you can create spells in your bathtub. Here are a few that use common everyday materials you have around the house:

- *Coins.* Drop a shiny coin into the bath for money spells.

- *Scarves.* Swirl a pretty scarf through the water to create a focus for your spell.

- *Candles.* Use floating candles to harness fire magic in your bath (be careful, though!)

- *Snow.* Melt some snow into your bath to give thanks for the winter months.

- *Rainwater.* Add rainwater to spell for water for the world.

- *Time.* Bathe at different times of the day for different magical effects. Try a moon bath with a moon stone and a few drops of moon water, or a sun bath with a citrine and some sunflower petals.

- *Clover.* Add clover leaves for luck.

- *Salt.* Use salt in your bath before magical rituals to cleanse the body and spirit.

After a magical bath, try, if you can, not to dry yourself off after you get out. Simply wrap a towel or bathrobe around you and dry naturally. Scrubbing at yourself with a towel can remove a lot of the magic you have just bathed in. Besides, drying naturally is a lot less work!

Inner Voices

Because you spend more time in your home at this time of year, consider devoting a little more time (hopefully) to yourself. Our development on our own magical paths is something for which we all need to take responsibility—whether we are just starting out or have been practicing for years. That inner voice we all have needs to be heard. Is it shouting at you for some peace, because your thoughts are going twenty to the dozen, as mine invariably do? Is it calling for more knowledge? Does it want you to connect with it and just accept that it's there?

It is not easy to hear your own thoughts over the din of everyday life and all it takes to get through a day. But sometimes, that inner voice just needs to be nurtured. You may find that reading helps, and certainly the Internet is awash in ways to answer our thoughts and questions. But the work that will really make the most difference to your inner voice is meditation.

Finding time for meditation can be the least of your worries. Meditation just doesn't come easily to some people, myself included. I have to be honest. I have a brain that talks even more than I do, if that's possible. And for me, meditation can seem like a constant battle between thoughts and peace, with most of the time being spent telling myself that I should clear my thoughts in order to meditate. This leads to a cycle of my beating myself up and telling myself off for thinking that I should be peaceful, instead of just being peaceful. Do you follow my drift?

I have come to the conclusion that there is no right way to meditate. Just do what works for you. Remember, you are not a robot. You cannot turn your thoughts on and off like a tap—well, not unless you have had a great deal of practice, I think! All that being said, finding some quiet time to relax and listen to your inner voice is crucial to living a magical life. After all, your spells, rituals, and practices all come from within you.

Step-by-Step Guide to Meditation

It is your own focus and intent that creates magic. So trying to find your way through the map of your own mind has to be a good thing—right? There are many ways to do this. Some suggest lying on a bed and listening to a soothing whale song (awful). Some suggest sitting cross-legged on the floor (couldn't even if I wanted too, which I don't). Some suggest swaying to the hypnotic banging of a drum (would definitely put me off). Some say to imagine you're going down a flight of stairs (I always lose count of the stairs, start looking at the cracks in the imaginary wall, and think about redecorating). If any of these work for you, my lovelies, that's wonderful. Except the whale song—please don't do that!

None of these techniques work for me, however. So I needed to find another way to meditate, one that held true to my path and didn't pressurize my brain into thinking it had to be empty. Here's my step-by-step guide to meditation. I hope that those of you who are hopeless meditaters (like me) find it useful.

Find somewhere where you can connect with nature—the park on a spring day, the fields on a summer's eve, the woods on an autumn afternoon, your armchair facing the window on a wet winter's day. Sit or lie comfortably in the quiet and close your eyes. Take slow, deep breaths and listen to the sounds around you. Birds, wind, ticking clocks—anything that you can hear. Allow yourself to be absorbed by the sounds. Relax your body and feel yourself being a part of your surroundings.

In your head, begin to recite some simple words. I use: "I am part of nature." If thoughts come into your mind, acknowledge them, but try not to dwell on them right now. Decide to look at them later and return to hearing the sounds around you and thinking your chosen words. Don't feel as if you have to spend hours; just a few minutes will do to start. When you are ready to finish your meditation, stop saying your chant in your head and slowly become more aware of the things around you. Wiggle your toes and fingers, and open your eyes.

Practice this often, every day if you can. Try meditating in places other than nature. The bus or the coffee shop will give you a different experience. Don't beat yourself up or worry that you are doing it wrong. Your thoughts may come in for a reason, so allow yourself time to consider why you had those thoughts at the end of your practice.

Mind Maps

Meditation, when it works, is a wonderful way to journey into your own magical world. But, even if you are as hopeless at meditation as I am, you can still visit those magical realms of your mind. One of my favorite journeys is to travel in my head to my woodland grove. It's great there, and I think you would like it! There, I can carry out all sorts of magic and healing, talk to the Goddess and the Green Man, and find ways in which to reconnect with the magic of life.

You don't need to meditate to go on your own journey into your own grove. Just spend some time thinking about your own mind map. Close your eyes and see where you end up! You may be in a glade, on a boat, or in a meadow. Where does the Goddess reside in your world? What animals are there? Is there a beach in your mind? A lake? A mountain? Write down anything you come across on your mind travels in your Book of Shadows and research anything that is shown to you. Whatever you see is shown to you for a reason. Stones, animals, or paths will all have a purpose behind them. And don't forget to visit often. This is your world, only for you and your magical workings. How wonderful is that?

After all that journeying around in your mind, you'll need a bit of nourishment! This velvety chestnut soup is my favorite way to end a journey. It's soothing and warming, and will ground you after your travels.

Velvety Chestnut Soup

Ingredients

500 g./17.5 oz. fresh chestnuts or 2 packs of
whole peeled chestnuts

2 chicken or vegetable stock cubes

100 g./3.5 oz. grated potato

Bouquet garni bundle of bay, thyme, and parsley

8 tbsp. fresh cream

Salt and pepper

Fresh parsley, chopped, to garnish

Method

1. If you are using fresh chestnuts, boil them in a pan of water for a half hour. Cool them under running water and peel.

2. In a pan, add the 2 stock cubes to 2 pints of water and bring to a boil.

3. Add the chestnuts, grated potato, and herb bundle to the boiling stock. Reduce the heat and simmer for approx. 25 minutes, until the chestnuts are tender and the potato is cooked through.

4. Remove the herbs and purée the soup with a stick blender until smooth and velvety.

5. Return to a low heat and stir in half of the cream. Season with salt and pepper.

6. Ladle into bowls and top with a swirl of cream and freshly chopped parsley.

You can adapt this recipe to include any other vegetable you have around. Butternut squash works particularly well, as it complements the nuttiness of the chestnuts. Play around with the garnishes too. Chopped roasted chestnuts can be a great texture contrast, or try herby croutons.

ESSENTIAL OILS

Now that the winter has driven you inside, it is a good time to start to explore another form of magical working to expand your knowledge and develop your magical path. Something doubtless speaks to you—for some it may be crystals; for others it may be divination. One form of magical work that I particularly like is aromatherapy and the use of essential oils. This can be a really gentle form of magic, especially when used for healing.

You can buy essential oils in small bottles that contain the pure oil from the plant. They can be used in an oil burner for scent magic, or diluted with a carrier oil for massage, or added to spell bags or sachets to bring the plant's power to your spell. The best way to start using these oils is the same as with everything else—take baby steps and go slowly. Buy just one essential oil—lavender is always a good one to begin with—and learn all you can about the properties of that oil and how you can use it. Record all your research in your Book of Shadows, then use the oil in some simple spells and remedies at home.

There are so many essential oils out there that can lend you their magic. And you can use them around your home as well—just another way to make your home more magical! Add a few drops of your favorite oil to a couple of cotton balls and pop them into your vacuum cleaner for a wonderful scent when cleaning. Or sprinkle some drops on a damp cloth and add it to your dryer to add a beautiful fragrance to your clothes. Here are a few of my favorite ways to use essential oils in the home:

- *Lemon oil.* Use as a degreaser and sanitizer. Add a few drops to hot water before cleaning. You can also add a few drops to the toilet water to keep it fresh between uses.

- *Eucalyptus oil.* Use a few drops as a deodorizer when you wipe out the inside of your garbage can. Or add to hot water, then place a towel over your head and inhale the vapors as a remedy for a cold.

- *Peppermint oil.* Dilute with water in a spray bottle to spray anywhere mice may be a problem. They hate the smell.

- *Tea tree oil.* Spray a mist around the house to chase any bugs or germs away. Use it as a treatment for head lice, too.

- *Lavender oil.* Shake a couple of drops on your pillow to encourage a good night's sleep. And remember your dog's bed. Lavender relaxes animals as well!

- *Orange oil.* Wipe your fridge out with some to deodorize it. And give it a sniff to lift your spirits.

- *Rose oil.* Scent wrapping paper with it and use it to line your drawers. Cook with it and try adding a drop or two to your coffee for a North African flavor.

Witchy Ways to Celebrate November

- Decorate your home and altar with white and deep purple, and light incense of rosemary or nutmeg. Use a cauldron or pot with a candle lit inside as your focus of the hearth.

- Work with yourself! Find time to develop your own witchy skills, and take that magical bath.

- Cook with the last of the foraged ingredients before they disappear for the winter. Use winter vegetables and game to create seasonal meals.

- Connect with the Goddess in you by journeying into your own mind. Explore and take notice of all that you see there, and record all your discoveries in your Book of Shadows.

- Celebrate the darkness by drawing the curtains and spending time by candle-light.

- Make your home more magical using herbs and symbols, and research the folklore on home protection.

- Don't panic about Christmas. Admit it; you do it every year too!

November Folklore

"Thunder in November means winter will be late in coming and going."

"Frost in November to hold a duck, the rest of the winter is slush and muck!"

"Flowers bloomin' in late autumn, a sure sign of a bad winter coming."

"Ice before Martinmas, enough to bear a duck, the rest of the winter is sure to be but muck!"

Chapter Ten

———◆———

DECEMBER

In the darkness, the sun shines bright
Illuminating the land with its fertile light.
Winters still here and cold days will come,
But summers won't be long with the growing sun.

FOODS AT THEIR BEST IN DECEMBER

Fruits and Vegetables

brussels sprouts, carrots, celery, clementines, cauliflower, chicory, celeriac, cranberries, hazelnuts, Jerusalem artichokes, leeks, marrow, onions, pomegranates, parsnips, potatoes, quince, red cabbage, tangerines, turnips, salsify, satsumas, swede

Seafood

brill, cockles, cod, coley, clams, haddock, halibut, hake, John Dory, lemon sole, langoustine, monkfish, mussels, mackerel, oysters, pollack, plaice, squid, sea bream, skate, scallops, sea bass, turbot, sea kale

Wild Foods

chestnuts, chickweed, fairy ring champignon, duck, guinea fowl, goose, grouse (until december 10), hare, mallard, partridge, pheasant, sea purslane, sea beet, teal, turkey, venison, wigeon, woodcock, wood pigeon, wild rabbit, walnuts

December Correspondences

- *Festival*: Yule (winter solstice, Midwinter). Symbols include Yule trees and logs, holly and mistletoe, gifts and candles.

- *Moon name*: Cold Moon. Other names include Oak Moon, Frost Moon, Winter Moon, Faithful Moon, and Moon Before Yule.

- *Astrological signs*: Sagittarius, November 21–December 20; Capricorn, December 21–January 20.

- *Birthstones*: Turquoise and tanzanite.

- *Nature spirits*: Wood spirits and trolls.

- *Animals*: Deer and squirrel.

- *Birds*: Robin.

- *Trees*: Holly and evergreens.

- *Flowers*: Mistletoe, poinsettia, and hellebore.

- *Herbs*: Witch hazel, bay, and cinnamon.

- *Scents*: Cinnamon, cloves, and frankincense.

- *Colors*: Red, white, and green.

- *Goddess*: Cailleach Bhuer.

- *Powers*: Peace, light, and inner renewal.

- *Other*: The longest night, Christmas Eve, Christmas Day, Boxing Day, New Year's Eve.

Oh yes, it's finally here—the month that, when you were a child, took so long to arrive and, now that you're a grown up, comes hurtling toward you like an express train. December represents different things to different people, but there is no escaping this month. Just walk down any main street or past any window and your senses will be assaulted by twinkling lights and all things festive. Outside, the weather ranges from dark and gray to crisp and cold. Maybe even some snow?

If you are brave enough to venture out into the hedgerow in December, you will find—well, not much at all really. You may see a few animal tracks in the mud, or some tough old rosehips clinging stubbornly to their branches. But the star of the show in December, and really the only thing worth fighting through the weather to see, is the holly. Deep-green spiky leaves and brilliant scarlet berries practically shout at you to gather them and bring them home. And what would this season be without our prickly friend? Remember back in June when we were nattering on about the holly and the oak kings? This is the perfect time to celebrate the holly, before we get to the winter solstice, when it bows out of the battle and the oak king takes the throne. And speaking of battles, this is the biggest one of the year for me—and I bet it is for a lot of you as well. Yule verses Christmas! December seems to be the month for battles, doesn't it?

Round One—Yule

The festival of the Midwinter solstice falls on or around December 21—the time of the longest night of the year. At this magical time, the sun stands still in the sky and the nights start getting shorter again as the sun is reborn. Honest! It always seems strange to me that, when we're in the middle of a cold hard winter, the sunlight time is slowly getting longer. In the same way, it seems a little odd that the summer solstice marks the waning of the sun, just when, in our minds, summer has just started! The calendar that we live by these days sure seems to have things slightly wrong. I think our ancestors had the right idea—living by the seasons and the cycles of the moon and sun and not by numbers on a calendar. Certainly the builders of Stonehenge knew a thing or two about the sun and its movements. Let's face it, they built the most impressive of all the calendars that work with the turning of the Wheel.

Because the solstice is all about the sun, Yule is a festival of fire—a time to give thanks to the returning sun that will spread its warmth across the cold earth. The sun god is reborn of the Goddess. Many of the old traditions of Yule are still around today, under the guise of Christmas. The holly and the ivy are symbols of male and female forces, the prickly spikes of the holly being male and the soft entwining strands of the ivy representing the female. These evergreens were brought into the home at this time of year to represent the magic of the earth, symbolizing that it never dies, but merely sleeps.

Mistletoe was the most sacred plant of the Druids, and was traditionally cut from the mighty oak tree with a golden sickle, then caught in a sheet so that it never touched the ground. Druid priests then divided up the branches into small sprigs to share with the people, who hung them in their homes for protection and as a sign of goodwill.

Celebrating Yule can seem like a bit of an afterthought with all the Christmas trappings around us, but it is a wonderful time to take an hour out of the madness to focus on a really important part of the turning of the Wheel. I like to do this simple ritual on the evening of Yule. It gives me a chance to acknowledge the sun being reborn to us and to give thanks.

Yule Sun Ritual

You will need:

A candle to represent the sun—it can be a large candle, or one that is yellow, red, gold, or orange

Something with which to inscribe the candle—either your athame or a small knife, or even a toothpick or a needle

7 small candles, either birthday candles or tea lights, to represent the 7 other festivals of the Wheel of the Year

A piece of paper, coloring pencils or pens, and scissors

Sit somewhere comfortable with the candles in front of you. Arrange the smaller candles in a circle, leaving a space in the center for the sun candle. Take the sun candle and inscribe images of the sun into the wax. As you do this, chant:

Welcome sun, light reborn.

In thanks this candle I now adorn.

When you have worked your candle, place it in the center of the ring of smaller candles. Light the sun candle with the words:

Return of the Sun, the darkness is gone.

Light each of the seven small candles from the sun candle, saying with each one:

Blessed be!

Spend some time focusing on the sun candle and its place within the Wheel of the Year that you have created around it. Think of the light returning to the world and to your own life, spreading its warmth and energy into everything. Then take your paper and draw an image of the sun. Make it bold and bright by coloring it in. Cut out the shape carefully and write on the back of it: "The sun has returned, so mote it be!" Hold your paper sun aloft to the sun candle and say:

I create this sun with thanks and blessings.

If you can, allow your candles to burn down, or extinguish them with thanks. Relight the sun candle over the next few days to allow the magic of the returning sun to be part of your life. Use your paper sun as a focus for your Yule magic. Attach it to your Yule log, or thread it with ribbon and hang it on your Christmas tree to represent Yule in the festive celebrations.

The Sacred Yule Log

The Yule log was a big branch sought out for the specific purpose of taking center stage in the Yule celebrations. It was placed in the hearth and decorated with evergreens. Then it was anointed with mead, salt, flour, or oil and set ablaze with a piece of the previous year's log. Once the log had burned, the ashes were scattered around the home to protect the family.

These days, our Yule logs are mainly made of chocolate cake (yummy), but why not resurrect the tradition of Yule by making your own proper Yule log? It's a wonderful way to spend the afternoon in the fresh air and tire out those overactive kids and partners!

Forage and find a log around eighteen inches long. The length doesn't have to be precise; the right one will show itself to you. Gather natural decorations to adorn your Yule log. Look for pinecones, evergreens, nuts, berries, seeds, and feathers. Raid your storage cupboard for spices like cinnamon sticks, cloves, and star anise. Collect colorful ribbons or pieces of paper and some glue.

When you have collected all your items together, sit around a table with everyone who wants to be involved. Allow everyone to help decorate the Yule log, making it bright and cheerful. Wrap the ribbon around the log and glue all your decorations in place, until your log is transformed!

Once your log is decorated, give everyone a small piece of paper and a pen to write down their wishes. Once everyone has done this, fold the pieces of paper and tuck them in among the decorations and ribbons on your log. On Midwinter evening, take your log outside or place it in the fireplace and light it. As you do this, you can say a few words, like:

Yule log, Yule log, burning bright,
Wishes heard and granted this night.

If you don't want to burn your Yule log, use it as a wonderful seasonal centerpiece for your table. Surround it with candles to represent fire.

Round Two—Christmas

Ahhhh, the C word! Love it or loathe it, there is just no escaping Christmas, wherever you are. December 25 has the power to turn even the most sensible and levelheaded person into a gibbering wreck! That's why I have decided to include this day in my book. Whatever path you follow, you just cannot escape this holiday season. The run-up to the big day can be stressful and can bankrupt you in a flash, but the well-meaning thoughts of goodwill to all men keep us going—especially since, generally, the "all men" referred to are our very own loved ones.

Children take center stage at Christmas, as they are whipped to a fever pitch of excitement at the mere sight of a piece of tinsel and the thought of Father Christmas delivering all those goodies—direct from the TV advertisements to your tree, stopping only to raid your purse on the way through! My own two daughters were Christmas junkies—everything from the Coke ad to a fairy light had them whirling through December on a Christmas high. This could be contained while they were still at school, but as soon as the school holidays started, it became a losing battle.

The list of Christmas traditions in my house seems endless—from the specific date when the tree has to go up (the day after daughter number two's birthday), the chocolates coming out on Christmas Eve while I peel the sprout mountain, the mince pie and carrot for Rudolf at bedtime, and the 4 a.m. wakeup call of "He's been!" Then presents unwrapped at lightning speed, followed by a day of juggling an enormous turkey while sticking stickers onto various plastic toys. The Queen's speech and more food, all the way to Boxing Day, when the pile of leftovers must be tackled. I have crawled on my stomach across bedroom floors like a Christmas ninja to place stockings on beds and attended more Christmas school plays than I care to remember.

Why do we do it? It's all about the family, just as it was in the days before Christmas. We love them—dear old Grandma who's as deaf as a post, Mr. Silent and Sulky brother sitting in the corner with a beer, my poor neglected partner who seems to be getting more irritating by the minute, and our beloved children—bless them—with their high expectations and no patience.

We celebrate this time each year out of love. I don't follow the Christian path—as I expect some of you reading this don't—but I do have respect for others' beliefs. I believe in the Midwinter solstice, the festival of Yule, and the rebirth of the sun. And I celebrate it in my own quiet way as a Hedgewitch. I celebrate Christmas for my family and friends, for the coming together of us all, and for the intentions of peace to all men—however hard and sometimes unsuccessful that may be. I am nothing if not an optimist!

In so many families—including mine, I guess—Christmas is perhaps the only time of the year when we all sit down around a table and feast. There is no rule book to say you can't celebrate both Christmas and Yule. And for me, both are wonderful—especially now that I have my "oh-so-amazing and beautiful" grandbabies to spend them with. All the fun and none of the stress. I knew that not strangling my kids would pay off in the end!

Christmas Feast Pie

Ingredients for the pastry

225 g./8 oz. all-purpose flour

A pinch of salt

120 g./4 oz. butter

1 egg

1 tbsp. cold water

Milk for glazing

Ingredients for the filling

400 g./14 oz. turkey meat, cubed

225 g./8 oz. gammon, cubed

100 g./3.5 oz. fresh cranberries

1 small onion

1 tbsp. chopped sage

Salt and pepper

150 ml./5 oz. double cream

Method for the pastry

1. Sift the flour into a mixing bowl and rub in the butter until it resembles bread crumbs.

2. Add the beaten egg and water, and mix to form a dough.

3. Wrap in plastic wrap and place in the fridge to chill.

Method for the pie

1. Preheat the oven to 200°C/400°F.

2. Roll out just over half the dough and line a 20-cm./8-inch pie dish with it.

3. In a bowl, mix together the turkey, gammon, chopped onion, cranberries, and sage. Add the cream and seasoning.

4. Place the turkey mixture evenly on top of the pastry base.

5. Roll out the remaining pastry and place it over the top of the pie. Make two small slits to allow the steam to escape and brush with milk to glaze.

6. Place in the center of the oven and cook for approx. 1 hour 15 minutes, or until golden and cooked through.

7. Serve with brussels sprouts, roasted potatoes, and carrots.

Made with Love

Whether you celebrate Yule or Christmas—or both—this is the season to give gifts. The shops are overflowing with ideas for presents, but the best present you can give is one that you make yourself. Just as when we cast our spells, it's the focus and intent we put into the working that makes it magical, so a homemade gift means so much more because it carries your energy to the recipient. I have found that people are rarely disappointed with something handmade. They can feel the love and thought you put into their gift, and that makes it so much more personal.

Food always makes a nice present. But you can get crafty, too. It may save you some money, and you'll have fun doing it. Here are a few ideas:

- *Cards.* The shops are full of Christmas cards, but I'll bet you're hard-pressed to find Yule cards. Why not make your own to send out to family and friends? Keep them simple, unless you're a whiz with art. Include symbols of Yule like the sun, or holly. Write a short explanation in each card about the festival and why you celebrate it.

- *Holly cakes.* Bake a batch of simple shortbread and press a holly leaf into each piece before baking so that it leaves an imprint. Place it in a pretty bag with a tag explaining the tale of the holly and the oak kings.

- *Candles.* Decorate inexpensive candles with Yule evergreens to make centerpieces for your friends' tables.

- *Wreaths.* Forage for pinecones and berries and make small wreaths by tying them onto woven twigs.

- *Seasonings.* Fill jars with salt and add flavorings to create a gourmet seasoning. Lemon zest, pepper, and herbs all work well.

- *Bath oils.* Make simple bath oils. Use almond or olive oil as a base and add drops of essential oil.

- *Vouchers.* Create a voucher book of ways you can give of your time—babysitting, a home-cooked meal, a day's worth of gardening, etc. Your family and friends will be grateful to use them throughout the year.

- *Calendars.* Customize plain calendars with important dates and the festivals of the year.

- *Photos.* Frame photographs of you and your loved ones. Personalize the frames using natural nuts, seeds, and twigs.

- *Bookmarks.* Make your own bookmarks by folding paper, decorating it with something personal, and scenting it with essential oils.

BUILDING YOUR KNOWLEDGE

Whatever journey we may be on, we must always grow and learn as we go along. After all, there would be absolutely no point in standing still. That wouldn't be a journey at all—more like a bus stop! No one ever knows everything. And if people tell you they do, they are telling you porky pies. There is always more that we can learn, and building up your knowledge can be an amazing eye-opening experience.

You know what it's like if you spend any time at all on the Internet. You find one thing and it spirals off into something else, until you find yourself looking at something far removed from where you started! So once you have your core knowledge, how do you start building on it? Well, if you are going to build on anything, first make sure that the foundation is secure. No building is ever stable without strong foundations, and the same goes for your knowledge. Here are my tips for building up your knowledge. I hope you find them of some use.

- *Learn and review the basics.* You must make your basic knowledge part of your very core. This may seem a bit obvious, but I know, for myself, how quickly I can forget things. My memory isn't what it once was!

- *Decide what you need to know.* Once you have learned your basics and committed them to heart, think about whether there are any gaps in your knowledge that need filling. What is it that you really need to know? If your interest is in herbs, seek out information on anything you regularly use in cooking or magic. If your interest is in crystals, are there any that speak to you that you need to learn more about?

- *Cast a wide net.* Search a number of sources for the information you need to fill out your knowledge. Learn through word of mouth, books, and the Internet. Never trust just one source. Check and double-check any information you come across. If something doesn't resonate with you, trust your instincts and search some more. Use newspapers and the television to keep in touch with what's going on in the world. Someone or something out there may need your focus.

- *Plan your time.* Although I know it's sometimes easier said than done, set aside some regular time to nurture your knowledge quest. Even if you can only manage an hour every Sunday evening, then use it! Make the development of your path a priority on your journey, and take the time to focus on nurturing it.

- *Take things slowly.* Racing through new knowledge can be a dangerous thing, especially when it comes to magic. Remember, it is not a race. And the more time you take to do a proper job, the more likely that knowledge is to stick.

- *Record everything.* Write down, print out, or paint or draw everything you discover. Only by keeping a record of what you do will you be able to see how far you have come and give yourself a reference point for where you are heading.

- *Deal with your doubts.* Manage your doubts or questions as they come along. We all can be filled with self-doubt along the way. Nip it in the bud and look at what you have achieved. Try a simple meditation visualizing yourself holding a basket of knowledge. Keep this picture available in your mind whenever those doubts start to creep in. Remind yourself of why you love what you're doing.

- *Use what you learn.* One of the best ways to build on your knowledge is to practice what you've learned and see if it works for you. Knowledge is no good to anyone if it's not used, so practice as much as you can in your day-to-day life.

- *Focus on today.* Sometimes, especially when we first start out on our paths, we can become all-consumed with our thirst for knowledge. Keep it real and live life in the here and now—and enjoy!

Natural Soothers

So, does this time of year make you stressed? Stress is a little like a virus. It can spread like wildfire, and it's a rare person who doesn't get swept along on the stress-express train. When we're stressed and our defenses are a bit low, in swoops Mr. Illness and Mrs. Bugs and we're all set for a couple of months of battling our way through colds, sniffles, and anxiety!

December seems to be the catalyst every year for my lot. My beautiful, healthy, and calm family suddenly seems to turn into a howling mess of tissues and arguments in December. This year has been a particularly bad one for my "oh-so-amazing and beautiful" granddaughters, who have had bug after bug and numerous visits to the doctor. Their mother has had months of sleepless nights and tantrums from under-the-weather children. I do feel so, so sorry for her.

I am a huge advocate of modern medicine. After all, our ancestors would have jumped at the chance to be cured of simple ailments that, these days, we don't give a second thought. Back then, however, many simple illnesses could prove fatal. But I do believe that old ways and a bit of magic can do some good as well. So you may want to deploy some of these simple soothers in your home when the dreaded winter strikes and everyone's defenses have upped and run out of the door.

- *Lavender.* Drop everyone's stress levels down a notch by utilizing the king of stress busters—lavender. Defuse it into the air, add a few drops to a hot water bottle, a candle, or your pillows. It really does work to keep things calm.

- *Honey.* Always have a good supply of honey on hand. A teaspoon mixed with ¼ teaspoon of cinnamon taken regularly will knock out most colds. Honey and lemon drinks are soothing tastes of the summer, as are honey and milk.

- *Vitamin C.* Add plenty of vitamin C to everyone's diet. Citrus fruits and juices help the body fight off any bugs. Use lots of parsley, too. It's a great source of vitamin C.

- *Rose oil.* Be kind to your skin. Pamper yourself by making sure the biggest organ you have stays soft and nourished by moisturizing well after a relaxing bath. Add a few drops of rose essential oil to almond oil or your normal moisturizer to soothe your skin.

- *Herbal teas.* Try soothing blends like chamomile to ease any tension, or simply use hot water with lemon to cleanse away any sluggish feelings.

- *Breathe!* Slow, deep breaths will calm you if you're feeling fraught. Think a simple phrase while you breathe. I use "Gently soothe me, cleansing breath" over and over until I feel calmer.

- *Spices.* Cook with plenty of garlic, ginger, and chilies over the winter months. They are all wonderful at boosting your immunity, so bring on the curries!

- *Sachets.* Make a small pouch or sachet of thyme and eucalyptus and charge it with a simple spell, like: "Keep me safe and keep me well, keep me soothed I now do spell."

- *Warm it up.* Keep your environment comfortable by snuggling under blankets, lighting candles to represent the hearth, and placing bowls of water by radiators to humidify the dry air caused by central heating.

- *Chicken soup.* It is both warming and comforting, and has been proven to be effective against the symptoms of the common cold.

Using Spices in Your Home

This is the time of year when homes are awash with the scents of the season. And we tend to use spices in our cooking at this time more than any other. But these wonderful exotic goodies can be so useful around your home as well. Because most of them are bought already dried, spices are easy to store and can be kept on hand to use without notice. Here are simple ideas for how to use them:

- *Scent the air.* Make a simmering potpourri of cinnamon, cloves, and nutmeg to scent your home with festive smells.

- *Freshen the bath.* Make a pouch of star anise and cinnamon sticks to hang in the bathroom as a natural air freshener.

- *Protect your wardrobe.* Hang a bag of cinnamon, black peppercorns, and cloves in your wardrobe to protect against moths.

- *Repel pests.* Mix crushed peppercorns with flour and sprinkle the mixture around the base of your plants to stop those pesky bugs.

- *Fight mold.* Add ground cloves to warm water to wash away mold.

- *Neutralize odors.* Place your favorite spice in a bowl of water and microwave it until it boils. Allow it to sit for 15 minutes to neutralize any odors in your microwave.

- *Treat scalps.* Make an infusion by simmering ten bay leaves in water. Use as a finishing rinse to soothe your scalp and help treat dandruff.

- *Soothe stomachs.* Make a weak tea of turmeric and honey to help with an upset tummy.

- *Freshen breath.* Chew a cardamom clove to freshen your breath.

- *Relax joints.* Add crushed coriander seeds to your moisturizer and use it on any aching joints.

Wassailing

As December rolls to its end, it's time in the U.K. to roll out the tradition of wassailing. Traditionally, wassailing was like Christmas caroling that took place on New Year's Eve. People went from house to house singing to wish people good health. The wassail itself was a bowl of warming ale—or more traditionally cider, apples, and spices—that was topped with slices of toast. Wassailers drank it to warm them down to the tips of their toes. To earn a sip from this bowl, they sang wassailing songs at the door of the household.

Wassailing the apple orchard is a tradition that dates back to our ancient Pagan ancestors, but it is gaining popularity once again. A crowd of singers is led through the apple orchard by the King or Queen of the Wassail to the oldest tree. Once there, the king or queen dips a piece of toast into some mulled cider and places it in the branches of the tree to encourage favorable spirits and to ensure a good harvest. Then they pour more mulled cider around the base of the tree and bang sticks together and shoot guns to drive away all the evil spirits. Finally, the group serenades the tree with a wassail song:

> *Old apple tree, we wassail thee and hoping thou will bear,*
> *For who doth know where we shall be 'til apples come another year.*
> *For to bear well and to bloom well so merry let us be,*
> *Let every man take off his hat and shout to the old apple tree.*
> *Old apple tree, we wassail thee and hoping thou will bear,*
> *Hats full, caps full, three bushel-bags full, and a little heap under the stairs!*

What a wonderful tradition. Long may it continue!

Wassail Cup

Ingredients

2 ½ pints of good cider

3 apples, grated

60 g./2 oz. soft brown sugar

½ tsp. grated fresh ginger

½ tsp. grated nutmeg

2 cloves

1 cinnamon stick

Zest of a lemon

Method

1. Place half the cider in a large pan with the grated apples, and bring to a simmer to soften the apples.

2. Add the rest of the ingredients.

3. Heat through gently until warmed, ensuring the drink does not boil.

4. Remove the cinnamon stick and cloves.

5. Pour into a punch bowl and serve with a smile and a cheer for good health!

Witchy Ways to Celebrate December

- Decorate your home and your altar with red, white, and green, and with all things festive. Use holly, ivy, and mistletoe as your Yule focus; burn cinnamon, clove, or frankincense incense.

- Work with the family to create Yule decorations or a Yule log to add to your normal festive décor.

- Cook with foods that boost your immune system. Include sunflower seeds in your Yule foods to represent the sun.

- Connect with the returning light by burning a sun candle.

- Celebrate all things of the season! Recognize the festival of Yule as well as Christmas, but celebrate this time of year as a whole. Make it a time for family and friends to gather and have fun.

- Spend some time building up your knowledge and work on a plan to nurture your craft regularly.

- Be kind to yourself and others. Be aware of the stresses of the season and send out blessings for all those affected. Take time to be good to yourself.

December Folklore

"*The nearer the new moon to Christmas Day, the harder the winter.*"

"*If sun shines through the apple tree upon a Christmas Day, when autumn comes they will a load of fruit display.*"

"*A green December fills the graveyard.*"

"*If New Year's Eve night wind blows south, it betokeneth warmth and growth; if west, much milk and fish in the sea; if north, cold and storms there will be; if east, the trees will bear much fruit; if northeast, flee it, man and brute!*"

Chapter Eleven

JANUARY

Wassailing the trees for a bounty of fruit
It's time to gather for a bit of a moot.
Share songs and laughter at this time of year,
For spring's not far away we all cheer!

Foods at Their Best in January

Fruits and Vegetables

brussels sprouts, blood oranges, cauliflower, celeriac, cabbages, celery, chicory, cranberries, clementines, forced rhubarb, Jerusalem artichokes, kale, leeks, onions, pears, parsnips, potatoes, purple spouting broccoli, pomegranates, salsify, satsumas, shallots, swede, Seville oranges, turnips, walnuts

Seafood

brill, clams, cockles, halibut, hake, haddock, John Dory, lemon sole, mussels, oysters, sea bass, scallops, turbot, whelks

Wild Foods

chickweed, duck, goose, guinea fowl, hare, horseradish, mallard, oyster mushroom, partridge, pheasant, teal, truffles, venison, wigeon, woodcock

January Correspondences

- *Festival*: None this month.

- *Moon name*: Wolf Moon. Other names include Ice Moon, Old Moon, Snow Moon, and Moon After Yule.

- *Astrological signs*: Capricorn, December 21–January 20; Aquarius, January 21–February 20.

- *Birthstones*: Garnet.

- *Nature spirits*: House spirits and brownies.

- *Animals*: Fox.

- *Birds*: Pheasant.

- *Trees*: Pine.

- *Flowers*: Crocus.

- *Herbs*: Angelica and thyme.

- *Scents*: Pine, juniper, and musk.

- *Colors*: White and violet.

- *Goddess*: Freya.

- *Powers*: Protection, reversing, and undoing; clearing the decks; new ideas and goals.

- *Other*: New Year's Day, Wassailing, Plough Monday, Twelfth Night, St. Agnes' Day, Burns Night.

Hail and well met, January! Not much seems to be happening out there in nature does it? I think the words "cold" and "bleak" spring to mind. Yet joyful expectations abound as we head into a new year. So this is a wonderful time to give back to what seems to be a barren Mother Earth as she heads toward the dawning of spring. Share all that optimism with everyone and everything around you. It can be infectious!

Although most celebrate the New Year in January, we celebrated ours back in October, didn't we? But January, right or wrong, always seems to herald a new era. Who can fail to be swept along by the dawning of a fresh new year? And who can resist all the promise that a fresh new shiny calendar holds (mine always has cats on it). The new calendar, clean and pristine, is ready to be filled up with dates and arrangements—the perfect blank slate!

January is still, for me, a time of fresh starts—as I expect it is for a lot of you lovelies. Hope, hope, and more hope for a wonderful year to come. All across the land, the words "Let's hope it's a better year than last year" resound in so many households. The word "hope" certainly seems to be the watch word for January.

In the house, holiday decorations come down and suddenly everything looks a little bare, reflecting well what's outside the window. The winds are cold and there is more chance of snow, which gets everyone in the U.K. excited, because we so rarely get the white stuff these days. Hangovers from New Year's Eve celebrations aside, we launch into the month with strength, will power, and a hell of a lot of fingers crossed as we tackle our New Year's resolutions. Oh, how many have I made over the years! I will be five stone lighter, healthier, better off, happier, and kinder. I will not swear, else money goes into a swear jar. I will only put into my body wonderfully fresh and organic food; I will nourish my soul. And I will become Super Mum—no more shouting for me!

These amazing resolutions seem so doable on the first of January. New year, new start, what will power I have! Then the second of January dawns and will power ebbs, and by the third of January, I am swearing like a fish wife, gorging on chocolate, and blowing the entire week's budget on a fast-food dinner just to shut everyone up—including my own brain! It is a fact of life that we all, at one point or another, fail in our resolutions, mainly because we make them so unrealistic and are so hard on ourselves. It does make me wonder why we do it every year. We set ourselves up for a lousy January before it even starts!

I think that tempting blank calendar is to blame—pages of empty spaces just waiting to be filled with hope. I have found a way to fill mine with hope at the start of the year, instead of making resolutions I know I can't keep. On January 1, I sit in front of the new calendar and fill in all the family's important dates—school holidays, birthdays, etc. Next, I fill in all the festivals, full moons, and magical dates I observe. Then I fill in one key word a month for the entire year; these act as my focus for each month. I use words like "sun," "herbs," "baking," "trees," etc. By doing this, I give myself a month of working with each word, as a learning time during which I expand my knowledge and give thanks. These are my magical goals. I find that this gives me a calendar full of hope and a promise of a magical year to come. So much easier than having no focus at all, and certainly easier than making unrealistic resolutions.

Now I must share with you all my worst New Year's Day ever! A few years ago, Mr. Hedgewitch, daughter number two, and I went with my in-laws to a New Year's celebration at the local hotel—dinner, dancing, and lots of lovely wine. It was a fabulous night! We went back to their house to spend the night. The next morning, we woke late and got ready to leave for home. With a bit of a bang, my little old junker of a car decided to shed its fan belt as it started up. After quite a long wait for the repair man, along came a lovely, jolly, rather large gentleman who found the problem and swiftly fixed it. He moaned all through the repair, however, about what an awful car mine was to fix, as it was so small.

Well, finally we got into the car once again and set off for home, via the petrol station. With some fuel in the tank and only three miles left to go, we pulled back onto the road and—snap, the clutch broke. Not knowing whether to laugh or cry, we called the repair service again and, after a few hours of hanging around in the absolutely freezing cold, gray day, the repair man arrived. Of course, it was the same man who had rescued us earlier—and not exactly over the moon to see us again, or the car. However, this story does have a happy ending. That lovely large repair man spent a couple of hours flat on his back under my extremely small car in the freezing cold, just to fix my clutch so we wouldn't be left carless. I am still, to this day, very grateful for what he did. But wow! Not exactly a dream start to the new year, eh?

Now, a wonderful way to set yourself up for a magical year is to perform a simple spell on New Year's Day—if you're not stuck by the side of the road with your car, that is—or as close to New Year's Day as you can. This allows you to set the Wheel of the Year in motion for you and gives you a strong positive focus for the magic of the year to come.

New Year's Vow

You will need:

A simple white candle

16 small sheets of paper and a pen

An envelope

Pine needles—use some from your Christmas tree if you have a real one

A flame-proof dish

Sit somewhere where you feel comfortable. Start by closing your eyes and taking slow, deep breaths. Focus on the feeling of joy and hope as you start the new calendar and a new chapter in your magical journey. When you are ready, take your paper and pen and draw symbols that represent the Wheel of the Year on each one. You will need eight symbols, each drawn twice, to make up sixteen symbols in total. Use images that are meaningful for you. Here are some ideas:

Imbolc: a candle

Ostara: an egg

Beltane: a May pole

Litha: the sun

Lammas: a corn sheaf

Mabon: an apple

Samhain: a pumpkin

Yule: a Yule tree or log

Focus on the Wheel of the Year as you draw, and on how you will celebrate and honor each festival. Once you have two of each symbol, make two piles of the Wheel of the Year in front of you. Light your candle and say:

Scared flame of light I ask,
Aid me in my magical task.

Take the first pile of drawings and look at the first image carefully. Then say:

I vow to myself and Mother Earth to observe Imbolc and
celebrate the Wheel of the Year.

Carefully set light to the drawing and place it in the flame-proof bowl. Sprinkle the burning paper with a few pine needles, saying:

Sacred pine of brand new start,
I make this vow with all my heart!

Do this with all the pieces of paper in the first pile, using each festival name and sprinkling each burning layer with pine needles. Once all eight drawings have been burned, hold your hand over the bowl and say:

Hear my vow, so mote it be!

Then take your second pile of eight drawings and place it in the envelope. Sprinkle in some pine needles and seal the envelope. Hold it between your hands and say:

May this packet be a reminder for me.

Allow your flame to burn away safely, or extinguish it with thanks. Take your bowl of burned drawings and pine needles and bury it outside to cement your vow to Mother Earth. Keep your envelope somewhere where you will see it every day as a reminder of your promise to yourself. Next New Year, you can burn it and create a new packet.

LETTING GO AND STARTING OVER

There are always times, whether it's New Year or not, when we have to let go of something that's not working. Letting go of anything that's become dear to you can be so hard. It can leave you feeling lost and out of balance with everything. As we travel on our journeys through this life, we will all have to face letting go of something. And with that fresh start, we face the challenge of a new way of living. The world around us is constantly changing. What may have been right for us or felt important to us in the past may not now have a place in our lives. Sometimes, the decision to leave things behind can be a hard one to make. So how do you know whether you are making the right decision to move on and let go?

If you are magically traveling your path, here are a few things you may want to consider as you leave things behind:

Is someone or something having a negative effect on your life?

Have you outgrown something, or grown apart from something?

Are you happy in your life as things are? Have your goals changed?

Do you live in the past? Hold a grudge? Are you in fear of things being different?

Are your needs being fulfilled? If you are starting on a new path, is something holding you back?

Only you can know whether it's time to let go of something. It's a bit like smoking, I suppose. Unless you really want to give it up, no amount of advice or knowledge is going to help you. But it may help you make your own choice. Listen to your heart. Inside, you will know if it's right for you to move on and start over. As you do, it may be worth considering some of these thoughts:

Accept that things need to change in your life in order for you to live the way you need to and embrace a new path.

Take a step back and focus on what you really want and need—what will help you in the future.

Look inside yourself, and not to others, to move on. Be guided by your own beliefs and needs.

Take a chance—and a deep breath! That first move in letting go and starting over is the most terrifying. It will only get easier with time.

Be thankful for your past, but focus on today and keep moving ahead. It's your future.

You can only walk so far with a backpack full of burdens. Set it down, sort through it, and then move on. You will feel lighter and freer!

Wow! How heavy was that for me? But I hope someone out there found it useful. Let's face it, we all have to leave things behind and sometimes start again. Change can be one of the joys of life! But after all that thinking, maybe it's time to hit the kitchen and break that no-chocolate resolution!

Diet-Can-Wait Chocolate Pudding (serves 4)

Ingredients

2 tbsp. corn flour

25 g./1 oz. caster sugar

300 ml./10 oz. milk

Zest of an orange

100 g./3.5 oz. plain chocolate

150 ml./5 oz. double or whipping cream

Grated chocolate and cocoa powder to decorate

Method

1. Mix together the corn flour and sugar with a little of the milk to make a paste.

2. Heat the rest of the milk to just under boiling and remove from the heat.

3. Stir in the corn-flour mixture and return to the heat.

4. Keep stirring the mixture until it starts to thicken, around two minutes.

5. Break up the chocolate and stir into the sauce with the orange zest. Stir gently until the chocolate is melted.

6. Remove from the heat and cover with damp waxed paper until cooled.

7. Whip the cream to soft peaks and fold into the cooled chocolate mixture.

8. Spoon into 4 serving bowls and top with grated chocolate and cocoa powder.

PEOPLE ON YOUR PATH

So you have made the decision to follow a magical path. Maybe it's one you made many years ago, or perhaps you are coming new to your journey. It's really easy to think about the tools of the trade—wands, cauldrons, etc. But what is it that you actually need to follow the magical way?

I believe the only thing you really need is *you!* Your heart and a soul that sings with joy of the world is the most valuable tool you can possess. Now, no one can skip through life without a care. That would be so unrealistic. Running a normal everyday life brings with it chaos and changes, worries and fears. We are all only human. But in those small daily moments of magic, does your heart fill with love and kindness? Does it focus precisely on the task at hand? Do your eyes see the beauty of a rainy day, and do your feet want to trample through the snow to get a closer look at the robin?

As someone who has followed a gentle magical way of life, I know that I sometimes have to take a step back and look at things anew. I need to refresh my feelings of joy in the world and everything around me. No one is perfect, and certainly not me—but my intentions are true!

You are the most magical of tools. All your magic starts with you. Believe in yourself and your heart and you will have everything you need to travel on your journey and be fulfilled. If you have traveled this magical path for many a moon, take time often to rededicate yourself to your path. Remind yourself of why you started and celebrate all you have learned. If you are new to this way of living, focus on that amazing feeling of a new adventure and hold it dear to you. Remind yourself of it as often as you can. It really helps keep that wonder and awe alive in your life.

Family and Friends

We all need our family and friends; we love them. But they won't necessarily be of the same mind as we are. In fact, most family members will have their own view of what you are doing. At the start, they may express their doubts loudly and clearly. It can be hard when those close to you disagree or don't understand your passion. And it can be easy to judge—which is precisely what may be happening to you!

If you change who you are and how you live, even in the most subtle of ways, your loved ones will notice and may buck against this new you. It is unreasonable to expect others to change just because you are changing. So the best thing you can do in any situation in which your beliefs are questioned is to answer openly and honestly. For children's questions, keep things simple and filled with circumstances that they can see and relate to. For partners or family and friends, always answer any questions gently.

Stay true to yourself and your beliefs, but don't thrust anything down people's throats! You may be filled with excitement about your magical ways, but your loved ones may find them frightening and strange. Keep you magic low-key and soft when at home with others that share your space. You can cast spells and perform rituals simply and without massive fuss and ado. Keeping things normal at home is easy when you use the everyday things around you to practice your magical ways.

Neighbors and Towns

We are very fortunate in the U.K. to live in a mostly understanding country. People of all beliefs reside here peacefully and considerately, for the most part. But there can be exceptions. This may be because of our ancient history and the ways in which it is preserved here even today.

I do know, however, that the same cannot be said for all areas of the world. There are some people outside our own circles who will look upon any magical way of life as strange, unknown, evil, or bad. If people have no understanding of what you are doing and you are wafting around town casting spells and jangling crystals, they may, quite rightly, be scared. If your window is suddenly covered with pentacles and wands, it may spark gossip and wariness. And, as we all know, there isn't much that is more damaging than small talk.

So what do you do? Well, it's all a matter of personal choice, I guess. You know where you live and the people around you. I have no problem walking around Avebury Henge in my cloak with my basket, celebrating all things witchy. But I wouldn't necessarily go shopping in the same get-up. Am I ashamed of what I am? Certainly not! Nor should you be. But it is wise to judge how you carry out your magic around others. I sometimes get questions about my pentacle necklace or bracelet, and that can be a good thing, because it opens the doors of conversation, which can lead to understanding.

It's actually amazing how interested other people are in what we do. So if people ask you questions, try answering them with questions of your own. Maybe their grannies had certain remedies or traditional practices that they would like to share with you.

The Whole Wide World

We are part of a global family—which can be hard to remember in these days when we live so sheltered from one another. Beliefs that fall outside the standard religions are growing in popularity—and growing fast! So how can we, as mainly solitary practitioners, connect with events out there in the big wide world?

You only have to look at the Internet in times of crisis to see the spread of blessings and prayers sent out to those in need. Make yourself part of the healing energy that is spilling out from all of us to those in need of strength and help. If you read or see something that calls for a response, respond! Light candles; focus on healing. When you do, you become part of a network of energy that grows by the day. You may be only one person, alone in the bedroom with a tea light and good intentions. But all of us together can make such a difference in the world. We can make it a more magical place again.

Mummers' Plays

January is the traditional season for mummers plays, also known as mumming. These are old folk plays performed by actors known as mummers or guisers (performers in disguise). They originally came from England but can now be found all over the world. Today, these plays are most often performed in the street, but they used to be performed as house-to-house visits and in pubs. The term "mummers" has been used since medieval times, and may have been used to describe many different kinds of performers.

The earliest evidence of mummers plays as they are known today is from the mid- to late 18th century. A key element of the tradition was visiting people in disguise at Christmas and New Year. The plays were usually comedy performances, and generally involved a battle between two or more characters, representing good against evil. Usually, they featured a doctor who had a magic potion that could resuscitate a character who had been killed.

In mummers plays, the central plot is the killing and bringing back to life of one of the characters. The principal characters are a hero, his enemy, a fool, and a quack doctor. The most important character is the doctor, and the main purpose of the play's conflict is to provide him with a patient to cure. The hero sometimes kills and sometimes is killed by his opponent. But whoever is slain, the doctor comes to restore the dead man to life. The name of the hero is most commonly Saint George, King George, or Prince George. His enemy is a dragon or a Turkish knight. Other characters include Old Father Christmas, who introduces some plays; Little Devil Doubt, who demands money from the audience; and Robin Hood, Prince of Thieves. These wonderful traditional plays are making a comeback in the U.K. and are worth watching if you get the chance. Or you can make up your own with your friends and family. What a brilliant tradition to start—or rekindle!

Thanks and Blessings Every Day

Mummers plays are seasonal rituals that bring magic to life. But any daily ritual can become the cornerstone of your own magical practice. It doesn't have to be long and drawn out, nor do you need lots of materials for it. A ritual is just an action that you perform regularly, so it is a wonderful way to send out thanks and blessings every day. As you know, I like to keep things simple, so this is my daily ritual. You will need:

> 3 candles—one for the Goddess, one for the Lord of the Greenwood, and one for all sentient beings
>
> An incense stick, or loose incense and a charcoal block
>
> A few grains of salt
>
> A few drops of water
>
> A bowl to act as your offering bowl

Sit comfortably in front of your altar or at a sideboard or windowsill. Safely set out your three candles in a row in front of you. Light the middle one, as you say:

> *I light this candle in the name of the Goddess,*
> *with thanks and blessings this day.*

Then using the flame from the Goddess candle, light the left-hand candle and say:

> *I light this candle in the name of the Lord of the Greenwood,*
> *with thanks and blessings this day.*

Light the right-hand candle from the flame of the Goddess candle and say:

> *I light this candle in the name of all sentient beings,*
> *with thanks and blessings this day.*

Next, light the incense stick in the flame of the Goddess candle (or light the charcoal block and sprinkle on the incense) and say:

With the power of air, I light this incense with thanks and blessings.

Then take a few grains of salt and add it to your offering bowl, saying:

With the power of earth, I offer this salt with thanks and blessings.

Add a few drops of water to your offering bowl and say:

With the power of water, I offer this water with thanks and blessings.

Hold the bowl over the incense smoke and above the candles, saying:

Blessed be!

Spend a few moments with your thoughts and your ritual is done. Leave your candles to burn away safely, or extinguish them with thanks. You can use the same candles for your ritual each day if they can stay in place. Empty your offering bowl into the earth whenever you feel the need.

You may notice that I use the words "all sentient beings." This is a term that my dear friend, Robert, taught to me, and I am very grateful for it. *Sentient* means "able to perceive or feel." I think it is a wonderful way to include everything in the universe, even if we don't know of its existence yet, don't you?

Passing on Knowledge

I love it when I get to learn something passed on by someone else—like that term "sentient beings," passed on to me by my friend Robert. Passing on our knowledge is really rewarding—like when you pass on the recipe for an amazing cake you have made. But it is also absolutely vital for keeping our ways alive. Our ancient ancestors didn't really have the means to record their daily lives and practices, and word of mouth has died out over the last century as communities have changed. So how do we pass on our knowledge to the generations to come?

First, we need to start close to home, with our own children and grandchildren. They will carry our knowledge forward to the next generations if we share our ways with them. Our tales will become the tales of the ancestors one day. How cool!

So talk! Speak about home remedies, herbs and plants, magic and Mother Earth as soon as the little ones are old enough to listen. Tell them any old tales, nursery rhymes, and folklore and it will be carried forward. It may be of very little use to talk to a moody teenager who thinks everything that comes out of your mouth is boring. But if you delight and enthrall them while they're young and interested, you may win the battle. Show them how to temper the sting of a nettle with a dock leaf. Show them how to leave offerings for the Fae folk. Show them how you knead bread. Show them everything and watch as they absorb it—like little sponges.

Another way to pass on our knowledge is, of course, to write it down. Books of Shadows, scrap pieces of paper, anything that will record and document your knowledge for the future is valuable to everyone. And don't forget the Internet. Blog, comment, and get involved in the exchange of knowledge. One of my favorite things in running the Hedgewitch Cooks website is the exchange of knowledge that comes when people respond to the posts. I have learned so much that I have recorded for the future, and I hope I have passed some knowledge on as well. Can you imagine the wealth of traditions that have been built up already on the World Wide Web? I can tell tales from the countryside of Wiltshire and hear tales from around the globe. New traditions are blending with the old and creating a new system of values and beliefs that move with our modern times. And as a thoroughly modern Hedgewitch, I say hurrah!

Sigil Magic

Sigil magic is a really wonderful way to cast spells. It is done by simply writing down what you wish to spell for, condensing it into a symbol or picture, and then making that picture even simpler. You end up with a unique drawing made from the words of your spell, which will be a powerful image for your subconscious mind. Here's how you can make a sigil spell.

First, write down your sentence. For this example, we will use:

I spell for peace for the world.

Next, cross out any letters that repeat. Our sentence here will look like this:

I Sxxx xxx xxACx xxx THx WxxxD

This leaves the letters:

Once you have simplified your statement and gotten your letters, you can then make up an image by linking the letters to make a picture. It doesn't matter how you do it, just simply place the letters to form a symbol. Once you have your symbol, simplify it further by removing some lines to create a really basic image. This is your sigil.

Charge your sigil as you would your herbs. Once it is charged, you can then tuck it away and not think about it. The magic has been set in motion.

Think of new ways to use sigil magic. For example, use natural food coloring to paint your sigil on your body before taking a bath to promote healing. Or scribe it into a pastry before baking and eating it. Sigils are a great way to cast simple spells.

Oats and Flour

Oats and flour are two staples that everyone should have in the home. They ground us in the earth element and remind us of the turning of the Wheel of the Year. Here is a simple recipe for breakfast rolls that can bring magic into your day.

Oaty Easy Breakfast Rolls (makes 12)

Ingredients

400 g./14 oz. whole-meal flour

100 g./3.5 oz. oats, plus some for sprinkling

1 tsp. salt

2 tsp. baking soda

300 ml./10 oz. water

150 ml./5 oz. natural yogurt

4 tbsp. vegetable oil

4 portions of cooked bacon

2 tbsp. chopped chives

Method

1. Preheat the oven to 190°C/375°F.

2. In a bowl, mix together the flour, oats, baking soda, and salt.

3. Chop the bacon and add this to the dry ingredients, along with the chives.

4. In a separate bowl, mix the yogurt, oil, and water.

5. Mix the wet ingredients into the dry, until the mixture is thoroughly combined.

6. Split the soft dough into 12 sections and shape roughly into rounds.

7. Place on a baking sheet lined with waxed paper.

8. Sprinkle the top of each roll with a few flakes of oats.

9. Bake in the oven for around 15 minutes, or until golden brown and hollow-sounding when tapped on the base.

10. Leave to cool slightly and serve warm with plenty of butter.

Top Tip for Oats and Flour in the Home

It's not just in your recipes that you can use oats and flour. Here are some tips for using these two favorite kitchen staples.

- *Facials.* Use a mixture of honey and oatmeal as a face mask to calm your skin.

- *Baths.* Add oats to your bath to soften your skin.

- *Air freshener.* Leave oats in the fridge to absorb bad odors.

- *Play-Doh.* Make homemade Play-Doh by mixing two parts oatmeal, one part flour, and one part water. Color with a few drops of natural food coloring and get crafting!

- *Cleaner.* Clean stainless steel with dry flour and elbow grease to bring up a lovely shine.

- *Pest repellant.* Sprinkle your vegetable plants with flour to deter pests. Use it as an ant powder to form a line of defense to keep them out of the house.

- *Fire extinguisher.* Keep flour on hand in case of a stove-top fire. Sprinkle on any splashes to get fires under control.

- *Glue.* Make a homemade, nontoxic glue by mixing one part flour to three parts water. Place in a saucepan and bring to a boil. Simmer for three minutes, stirring till smooth and thickened.

Witchy Ways to Celebrate January

- Decorate your home and altar with violet and white, and burn pine and musk. Use pine needles as your focus for new beginnings.

- Cook with love and try new things to add a spark to the new year.

- Honor your place in the world and the joy in your heart by creating a daily practice.

- Try a new way of spelling by creating a sigil.

- Let go of what's not working for you; start with a clean slate and move on.

- Create a magical calendar for the year and give yourself a focus for each month.

- Be understanding of others' beliefs and promote your own in a sensitive, open way.

- Fall in love with the world around you again as you get ready for the first stirrings of spring. The earth is at its barest—warts and all—so celebrate any beauty you find.

January Folklore

"Here's to thee, old apple tree whence thou mayest bud, whence thou mayest blow, whence thou mayest bear apples enow."

"January brings snow, makes our feet and fingers glow!"

"To shorten winter, borrow money due in spring!"

"Pale January lay in its cradle day by day, dead or living hard to say."

Chapter Twelve

—◆—

FEBRUARY

Little snowdrops glowing white
Filling us with first spring light.
In the hedgerows you herald spring,
Listen close and you will hear them sing.

Foods at Their Best in February

Fruit and Vegetables

brussels sprouts, blood oranges, chard, cabbages, celeriac, cauliflower, endive, forced rhubarb, Jerusalem artichokes, kale, leeks, Medjool dates, onions, parsnips, pears, pomegranate, potatoes, red chicory, radicchio, parsnip, purple sprouting broccoli, swede, walnuts, turnips

Seafood

brill, clams, cockles, halibut, hake, haddock, mussels, oysters, sea bass, scallops, salmon, turbot

Wild Foods

alexander (horse parsley), chickweed, horseradish, hare, nettle, venison (slim pickings in the hedgerow!)

February Correspondences

- **Festival**: Imbolc. Symbols include candles, the Brighid cross, lambs, bulbs, and milk.

- **Moon name**: Hunger Moon, due to the lack of food at this time of year. Other names include Snow Moon, Trappers' Moon, Storm Moon, and Moon of Ice.

- **Astrological signs**: Aquarius, January 21–February 20; Pisces, February 21–March 20.

- **Birthstones**: Amethyst and rose quartz.

- **Nature spirits**: All air spirits and young earth Fae.

- **Animals**: Moles, badgers, and sheep.

- **Birds**: Owls and herons.

- **Trees**: Willow and hazel.

- **Flowers**: Snowdrop, crocus, violet, and aconite.

- **Herbs**: Rosemary and sage.

- **Scents**: Pine, sage, and violet.

- **Colors**: White, green, and silver.

- **Goddess**: Brighid.

- **Powers**: The stirrings of new beginnings; new energy and focus.

- **Other**: Candlemas, St. Valentine's Day, Shrove Tuesday (Pancake Day), Leap Year (every four years).

Let's face it—February is not the prettiest of months! The words "harsh" and "unforgiving" come to mind for me. It's one of those months that seem to have been slotted in as an afterthought by some enthusiastic calendar-maker of old: "Ummm, let me think . . . What shall I do with all these spare days? I know, let's throw in a little month of bleakness between January and March. No one will notice that there aren't enough days to make a full month. There! That solves the problem."

For me, however, February is my hopeful look at what's to come! Believe it or not, the first stirrings of spring are already beginning beneath the frozen ground. I know, I know. When it's blowing a gale and pouring with rain, it is really hard to imagine all that life just waiting below the surface. You have to have a certain amount of faith to believe that it's really there! All of nature still seems to be in hibernation (as am I).

Yet one day—quite suddenly, it seems—a green shoot appears! Hurrah! That one tiny hint of the coming spring can really lift you after what has seemed an end-less winter. Soon, snowdrops and primroses start popping up all over as the land awakens from its winter slumber. So, if February is a good time for Mother Nature to get out of bed and make an effort, then it's a good time for us to join her. Well, it would be rude not too!

February is a turning point for the Wheel of the Year. And it is host to the festival of Imbolc (Candlemas), which takes place on February 2. *Imbolc* literally means "ewe's milk." In February, this milk is being produced at lightning speed by sheep all across the land, getting ready to feed all those gorgeous bouncy lambs. It seems, from our perspective, that this is a harsh time of year for bearing children. After all, raising your newborn in a deluge of rain—or worse still, snow—is surely not a wise choice. But the ewes have it figured out. Their little ones are born with a nice woolly coat to keep them warm. And having them at this time in the year means that they will have the freshest and most nutritious spring grass available at weaning time. Now that's smart parenting!

Symbols for this time of the year are the Brighid doll and the plough. At Imbolc, the plough was traditionally decorated and anointed with whiskey to represent the preparation for planting the first crops of the year. Offerings of bread and cheese were left for the nature spirits and it was considered taboo to pick or cut any plant at this time. Each room in the home was lit with candles and a great feast was served. Young maidens made corn dollies, placed them on beds of white flowers, and carried them from neighbor to neighbor, who bestowed gifts on the image. It's probably just as well that this no longer happens, since I really can't see many girls today agreeing to wander up and down the street with a corn dolly in a basket. What on earth would that do to their street cred?

The word "February" is derived from the Latin *februa*, which means "purification and cleansing." Perfect! The first stirrings of spring and cleansing mean only one thing to me—time for a sort-out! Time to get things started. Time to look at the map of the road I am traveling and decide which direction to go. But first—at least if you're like me and can't do a thing without the words "I'll just finish this and then I'll . . ."—it's a time to put the kettle on. After all, who can achieve anything or make any decisions without a cuppa?

Happiness Is a Cuppa

A cup of tea or coffee—so familiar to us all! Certainly people barely get a foot through my door without the kettle going on. So this seems the perfect place to start! How many times do you make a cup of tea or coffee during the day? It is such a basic, ingrained ritual in all our households that we see it only as part of daily life and pay it little or no heed at all. But is it actually a ritual? I really believe it is. It's something that we do so often and probably something we do in the same way each time. How many conversations have taken place in your home, or someone else's, over a steaming mug? How many problems have been bashed out and emotions soothed by a hot cuppa?

Since this is a ritual that we perform all the time, doesn't it make sense to use it for some magical good? This is how to make a cuppa magically, with intent. And I have included a spell for happiness, as a cuppa rarely fails to bring a smile to my face. But you can make a brew for any purpose at all. Just change the happiness wording and the ingredients you use to something that is appropriate to you and your task.

Cuppa Spell for Happiness

So you make tea and coffee all the time, right? Of course! But this time, you will really focus on the ceremony of making it, and really use the brew for your magical benefit.

First, fuss a little. Start with a completely empty kettle. Fill it with clean, pure, cold water. As you do this, listen to the sound of the water filling the kettle. Hear the drops and splashes; feel the weight of the kettle increase. Put the kettle on to boil, and give thanks that you have the means by which to heat the water.

Select your very favorite mug or cup. Think about why it's your favorite. You may want to have a special mug or cup that you only use for magical purposes. Warm the teapot, if you are using one, or the cup if you are not. Feel and see the warm water move around the surface.

There is a huge variety of teas, coffees, and brews available today. Some are bought; some are foraged. But they all have their own magical uses and benefits. Chamomile for calm and peace, raspberry leaf for pregnancy, lemon and mint for refreshing and cleansing—the list is virtually endless. However, as this is a spell for happiness, you should use what makes you happy. If that's the finest loose tea, great! Herbal tea? Excellent! Tea bags or instant coffee? Use them! No one is going to be happy drinking something wonderfully natural and herbal if they don't like it and think it tastes like grass!

Now that your cup or mug and your beverage have been selected, it's time to make your happiness brew. Make your tea, coffee, or infusion with intent. Focus on all the elements that go into it. See the boiling water and feel the heat of the steam. Smell the aroma drifting up to you on that cloud of steam. (Not too close mind; don't burn yourself. That is not magical!) As you add any milk or sugar, imagine these elements combining with your drink, magically changing it into something you love and something that has been made to bring you happiness.

When you have made your drink, sit down! Try not to drift off to another task; bring your full focus to the cup in your hands. I can't tell you how many half-drunk cups of cold tea I find around the house. I love tea. But I so often get distracted and rarely get the time to finish a cup. What makes this moment so magical is the time you take to enjoy the experience.

Now imagine a feeling of happiness and comfort. Imagine that your cup is filling up with that feeling—fuller and fuller, until it overflows with all the happiness that should be within you! When you have found that feeling and your cup is overflowing with happiness, say:

Flow through me now

I ask of thee.

Replace all sadness,

So mote it be!

Sip your drink. Connect with its taste and warmth. Visualize it flowing from the cup into your body. Let the warmth of the drink spread joy, comfort, and happiness through your whole body, connecting every pore. Drink all of your brew; be focused and thankful for the happiness it is giving to you. Enjoy and savor the most run-of-the-mill thing most of us do so many times a day without thinking. Know also that the brew you have made with such focus and care will imbue every fibre of you with joy and happiness—down to the last drop! It really does work. Magic!

Enjoy your cuppa.

My Favorite Mug

Over the years, many, many mugs have come and gone in my house. I'm definitely not a cup-and-saucer person—too much room for error with all that balancing and fine china. Besides, I can never get my fingers through those tiny little handles.

I never really drank tea, and certainly not coffee, when I was young, although my mum seemed to live on strong black coffee—not really all that surprising living with me, Miss Moody teenager, and my brother, Mr. Silent and Sulky teenager! The first mugs that were officially "mine," I suppose, were not really mine at all. They were part of a set hired out to those starting up in military housing that came along with all the day-to-day basics. These unassuming mugs scared the life out of me. Every one of them represented a charge that had to be paid if it was so much as chipped. No relaxing cuppa to be had with them!

After I escaped from hired mugs, a collection of standard supermarket and charity-shop mugs started to creep into my kitchen cupboards. Many had various chocolate logos and fluffy chicks on them—ghosts of all those mugs full of Easter eggs that I bought for the girls over the years. I was never fortunate enough to have my own "mum mug" until a couple of years ago, when I received my first, my very own, proper mug! A birthday present from my brother, Mr. Silent and Sulky himself, this mug is quite tall and narrow, quite heavy, and has a duck-egg-blue glaze inside it. On the outside is a rhyme about what makes a great sister (clearly written about me) under the title "World's Greatest Sister" (so definitely about me, then). I absolutely love this mug, and it is perfect for coffee—but not for tea. I don't know why that is, but it just doesn't feel right for a cuppa.

Then, probably the greatest mug ever enters my life! It is white, not too heavy, and the perfect fit for my hand. It holds both tea and coffee comfortably and is always a comfort after a hard day. It has a pink bear on the front. But what makes it so special are the words emblazoned on it. Across the front of this perfect piece of crockery are the words: "Very Special Grandma." It was a Christmas gift from my "oh-so-amazing and beautiful" granddaughter, purchased on her behalf by my eldest daughter, as she was only ten months old at the time.

This mug is my favorite and most special mug because of the feelings it brings me each time I use it. I never fail to smile at the pink bear and the words on it. My husband is under direct threat that, if he so much as goes near my special mug, I'll—well, you know. I have seen far too many plates and cups fall out of his hands. Honestly, I have never come across anyone quite so clumsy!

So this is now my favorite mug—not a beautiful bone china antique, but a modern usable mug that fills me with joy, warmth, and happiness. And I wouldn't change it for anything. Now that's what I call magical!

 ## Sticky Honey and Date Tea Loaf

I make this recipe every February. Why? Because it takes me so long to get around to clearing out the cupboards after the dreaded (whisper) Christmas! Without fail, it seems that I always have half a pot of honey left over from glazing the holiday ham and a packet of dates no one wanted to eat. I really ought to stop buying them every year. But by the time we reach February, I need to use them up because I can't bear to throw them away.

This tea loaf is a perfect accompaniment to a good cuppa and is really quick and easy to make. You can charge your dates here for unburdening of concerns, which is perfect if you've got a friend coming over for a pot of tea and a moan!

Ingredients

175 g./6 oz. softened butter, plus extra for greasing

125 g./4.5 oz. honey

175 g./ 6 oz. light muscovado sugar

3 eggs

225 g./8 oz. self-rising flour

½ tsp. baking powder

1 tsp. ground cinnamon

1 cup of strong tea

100 g./3.5 oz. chopped dates

Method

1. Preheat the oven to 180°C/350°F.

2. Grease and line a 900-g./32-oz. loaf tin.

3. Soak the chopped dates in the tea for 10 minutes.

4. Set aside one tbsp. of the honey in a saucepan.

5. In a bowl, combine the butter, sugar, eggs, and remaining honey. Sift in the flour, baking powder, and cinnamon, and beat the mixture until smooth.

6. Drain any remaining tea away from the dates and add them to the mixture, stirring gently to combine.

7. Spoon the mixture into the prepared tin and smooth the surface.

8. Bake for 1 hour, or until well risen and a skewer inserted into the middle comes out clean.

9. Leave the loaf in the tin for 10 minutes to cool slightly, then transfer to a wire rack.

10. Warm the remaining honey over a gentle heat and brush over the still-warm loaf.

11. Slice and serve.

This loaf keeps really well and also freezes beautifully. Just wrap it up well and don't forget to label it. You have no idea how many suspect packages are lurking in my freezer!

The Land of Milk and Honey

In the normally gray, cold, and damp month of February, this phrase comes to mind for me. I know; I'm bonkers. But bear with me here. You're out walking the dog or on the way to school in the gloomy light of a normal day when, out of the blue, staring you straight in the eye, something brings you screaming into the realization that the world is awakening—a snowdrop, a primrose, a glimpse of blue sky, a bud on a tree. Wow! When did the world wake up again? I don't realize how long the winter is until this precise moment when nature slaps me in the face with a burst of new beginnings! It's hard, when in the tight grip of winter, to see anything but winter. But in February, you can suddenly see the land for what it really is, and what it can be. And, for me, that is represented by milk and honey.

Milk is associated with Imbolc (ewe's milk) and the white of the snowdrop. The rhythm of nature seems to flow in colors, and white is the predominant color at this time. Milk is the first life-giving food we all have as babies. It is the purest form of nourishment we have, and it's the item most often in our shopping baskets. We use it in our tea and coffee, in cooking and baking, or to drink neat or as a milkshake (chocolate for me, please). From this amazing fluid we get cream, butter, and cheese—all vital sources of the nutrients we need.

Did you know, however, that milk can be a really useful thing to have on hand around the home for medicinal, magical, and culinary uses? Here are some tips you may not know for using milk:

- *Non-slip bath oil.* Does your bath get slippery when you add essential oils to the water? Add the oil to a little milk before adding it to the bathwater, and no more slipping!

- *Burn and bite relief.* Soothe sunburn or insect bites by making a paste of milk powder and milk and applying it to the affected area. This paste can also be used as an effective but gentle makeup remover.

- *Skin softener.* Add milk or milk powder to a warm bath as a natural skin softener. (Cleopatra surely can't be wrong!)

- *Eraser.* Dip a piece of bread with the crust removed into milk, then wring it out and form it into a ball. Use it as a gentle eraser to remove marks from wallpaper.

- *Plant cleaner.* Wipe fresh milk on the leaves of your houseplants to free them from dust, and then gently dry. They'll love you for it!

- *Leather polisher.* Soak a cloth in fresh milk and leave it to dry. Use this to polish your leather shoes and bags for an amazing shine.

- *Stain remover.* Soak ink stains in milk to remove them naturally.

- *Flavor enhancer.* To make frozen fish taste "from-the-sea fresh," simply place it into a bowl of milk to thaw, then cook as normal.

Magically, milk represents the feminine and the mother, and so can be used in female or nurturing spells. Try making a comforting milk dish for a distressed female friend or relative. Milk also makes a wonderful offering. Leave a small dish outside, maybe under a blackberry bush, for the fairy folk.

Honey is truly a food of transformation. Those busy bee friends of ours collect all that lovely pollen from the flowers and transform it into amber gold. How clever are they? When the temperature reaches around 10°C/50°F, the lovely bees start making an appearance. So it's not unusual to see them waking from their sleep in a mild February.

Honey was used by the Egyptians in their embalming process, and has been used down the ages for its wonderful sweetness and medicinal properties. I know that, as a child, as soon as I had so much as a sniffle, out came the honey and lemon for me to drink, want it or not! If you take a look at a lot of the medical preparations for colds and flu, honey features heavily in them still. So reaching for the honey pot, like Pooh Bear, is exactly the right thing to do. Honey also features in the traditional drink of mead—perfect for all those celebrations.

Here are some other tips for using honey:

- *Preserve fruit.* Place fruit in a jar of honey. The anti-fungal properties keep your fruit beautifully and give the honey a gorgeous fruity flavor.

- *Sweeten foods.* Replace the sugar in your cooking with honey. Use less honey than you would ordinarily use of sugar. For example, if you use 1 cup of sugar, use ¾ of a cup of honey instead. Drop your baking temperature by 4°C/40°F too, as honey burns faster than sugar. And be aware that you may need to decrease the amount of fluids in your recipe. Experiment!

- *Enhance flavors.* Add a spoonful of honey to tinned or canned tomatoes to counteract the acid and bring out the flavor.

- *Cure colds.* For the dreaded cold and sore throat, drink hot honey and lemon, or mix honey with ground cinnamon and ginger and take a spoonful daily.

- *Ease hangovers.* Eat a spoonful of honey to help cure a hangover. The fructose speeds up the metabolization of the alcohol.

- *Help heal.* Apply a dab of honey to wounds, bites, and spots. It is the original natural antiseptic and antibacterial substance.

- *Soothe dry skin.* Mix a couple of spoonfuls of honey with the same amount of milk to make a nourishing face mask for dry skin.

- *Condition hair.* After washing, smooth a mixture of honey and olive oil through your hair and leave for twenty minutes before rinsing. This makes a wonderful natural conditioner.

Magically, honey can be used to add gentleness to spells. It is effective at drawing things toward you and sweetening the mood. It can also be used in money and luck spells. Make a simple honey infusion by gently warming it with some fragrant herbs. Sage, lavender, thyme, and rosemary all work really well and taste great.

Now, all this talk of milk and honey has given me the munchies. And I know just the thing for that!

Imbolc Instant Pizza (serves 2)

This is a wonderfully quick recipe—and I use the word "recipe" in the loosest of terms—to make for an Imbolc gathering. It's also a useful one to have up your sleeve for a quick children's tea, a light lunch or supper, or, in my case, a midnight munchies feast! It makes great use of feta cheese, which, of course, is made of sheep's milk and so represents the meaning of Imbolc. It also gives you a good excuse to get out and forage for the first time in the year, as you try to beat those bunnies to the first fresh dandelion leaves.

Ingredients

2 whole-meal pita breads

50–75 g./2–2.5 oz. feta cheese

8 slices of fresh tomato, or 8 sun-dried tomatoes in oil

2 tbsp. olive oil

Black pepper

A handful of fresh dandelion leaves, if you can find them;

   if not, rocket or watercress works as well

Method

1. Preheat the oven to 180°C/350°F.

2. Place the pita breads on a baking sheet and top with the tomatoes, then add the feta and drizzle with the olive oil. Season well with freshly ground black pepper.

3. Place in the center of the oven and cook for 15 minutes.

4. Remove from the oven and top with the dandelion leaves.

This is even good the next day for a packed lunch—if there's any left!

Time now for a little magic, methinks!

Candle Magic

Candle magic is one of the simplest forms of spell work you can do. So it seems to me that it's a great place to start learning the basics of spell casting. It doesn't require complicated rituals or lots of expensive magical tools, and it's something we have all grown up with. Remember all those birthday candles? This is probably something we have all done from a very early age; we probably don't even see it as a form of magic.

Candle magic follows the same principle as the birthday candle ritual, only instead of wishing for something, you say and visualize your intent. It can be as simple or as elaborate as you like. Here are some basics for performing candle magic.

Choosing Your Candle

You can choose any candle you like for your candle magic. Big or small, short or tall, fat or skinny—any candle that will work for you. Remember, it's your intent that makes magic happen! However, in most spell work, the candle needs to be burned completely. So if you use a jumbo long-lasting candle, you may be waiting for it to burn down for days! I certainly don't have the time or patience for that. Besides, some of those lovely big candles cost a fortune.

For me, I like to stay with what I know—birthday candles! They are reasonably priced, they come in a wealth of colors, and they burn away completely in five minutes or less. They are also easy to carry around for impromptu magic on the go, and most come with their own little holders that you can stick in the ground or in a bowl of salt for safety. If I need a longer-lasting candle, I use a tea light. They can also be picked up at little cost and last for between two and six hours, depending on the quality. Votive candles can be useful as well. I tend to use these to imbue the atmosphere at home—normally for peace, to counteract the chaos of everyday life.

If you can, always use a new candle for each spell you do. It's a good way to insure that your intent isn't tainted with the remnants of any previous magical workings or energies. This is, of course, unless you are doing an ongoing spell—say, healing for someone. Once your intent has been placed in a candle, it can be used for that purpose until the spell is finished or the candle is gone. I try to keep a store of candles for magical work ready in a small wooden box, hidden away from the sticky reaching fingers of the visiting little angels. I always go through the same process to get them ready for spell work, and it saves me time mucking around with each one before I use it.

To prepare my candles, I bury them in a bowl of salt and ask that they be cleansed of all debris they may have picked up along their way to me—whether it be physical or psychic energy. Remember, you never know who may have handled your candles before they reached your hands. And you really don't need the energy of someone's bad day at work interfering with all your good intent! After my candles are prepared, I place them all in my wooden box and I'm ready to use them as soon as I find a minute. Remember not to use this salt for anything else, as it will contain any negativity removed from the candles.

Color is also important in choosing your candle. Color magic can be used in a variety of ways, from cords to cooking. Using color in your candle magic can be fun, and it's certainly a great way to focus your intent. But it can also become complicated. Deciding what color candle to use can be a mine field. And what if you don't have the right color candle available? There is a simple guide in chapter 6 of this book that shows the colors I use for particular outcomes in magic and in all other workings.

If you're just starting out, however, you can always go with white. It's a color that's universally available and it is pure and untainted. And it's probably the cheapest color candle too! Using white candles allows you to start a spell immediately, without worrying about shopping for or finding the correct color candle. Let's face it. If you need to do a healing spell, it's not going to wait for you to run to the shops and frantically search for the right shade of blue!

Preparing for Candle Magic

You lie in a candlelit bath, scented with oil and purified with salt—peaceful and quiet while you focus your intent on the coming candle spell. Right? Oh, if only that were the case! However wonderful that may sound—and perhaps once in a blue moon it may happen—the reality of everyday life is that you have to be ready to put together and perform your spell at the drop of a hat!

Preparing yourself for candle magic is the same as preparing yourself for cooking—by washing your hands. So it's not the beautiful bath, but it does what is required. It cleanses away any unwanted energies or impurities. Give your hands a really good wash and really focus on the water washing away all the day-to-day grime and all the day-to-day energy. When you're finished and have squeaky clean hands, you are ready to start.

To anoint or not to anoint, that is the question! Anointing can be a really useful way of focusing your intent into the candle you are using. There are many anointing oils on the market, as well as many beautiful fragrant essential oils that you can use. Something may speak to you, or you may choose a favorite fragrance you associate with yourself or even with someone to whom you are sending healing. Occasionally, I do use something specific. But in general, I use the same basic vegetable, sunflower, or olive oil I use in cooking. I just decant the oil into a little jar that I use for magical purposes only.

To anoint your candle, simply take a drop of oil and rub it onto the candle, focusing on whatever your intent is to be. To draw something to you, rub the oil from the top to the middle and from the bottom to the middle. To send something away, rub the oil from the middle to the top and from the middle to the bottom. Try not to rub back and forth or round and round. This can make your intent very confused. And I don't know about you, but it doesn't take much for my mind to get muddled, let alone any focus I may have managed to achieve!

Inscribing your candle can also be a really useful way to focus your intent in your candle magic. This is what I do most often, I think. I have always had this strange fascination with melted wax. I love to play around with it, resulting in many a burned finger. I am definitely a fiddler, and there is something about scratching into wax that I find therapeutic. You can use anything for this task. Traditionally, people used their athames, but I like to use a pin or a toothpick. You don't have to be an award-winning artist for this. Just make a simple symbol or sign, or write a name. Remember, it's just a way of getting your focus into the candle and the spell at hand.

Performing Candle Magic

You've washed your hands, chosen your candle and prepared it, and you're all ready to go! Now for the most important thing in any form of magic—your intent. All of the things that we use day to day or specifically for magic are simply tools for your intent. Your focus and thoughts are what is truly magical in any ritual you perform.

The best way I have found to focus all my thoughts is simply to hold the candle in my hands and close my eyes. I then visualize exactly what it is I want this candle spell to achieve. For example, if I want to send healing to someone, I think about that person being well and healthy. If I need to increase my confidence, I imagine myself overflowing with confidence and stability. I imagine all these thoughts and images pouring through my hands into the candle I'm holding.

There is no time limit to how long you should hold the candle. Trust in yourself. You will know when the candle is ready; it will feel full of your intent. Place the candle in a proper holder so it can burn safely for however long it needs to. Remember that lots of hunky firemen aren't going to help you in your spell casting, however gorgeous they may be!

Light your candle, keeping all your intent and focus on it. Try not to drift off to thinking about what's for tea. Once your candle is lit, imagine its flame transforming your intent and carrying it up and out into the world. If you can, leave the candle to burn down safely to complete your spell.

If you can't leave your candle to burn down safely, what do you do? If you are a really prepared and organized person, you will have selected a candle with the correct burning time for your spell, allowing you to be present throughout the whole burning time. This is not me! Rarely am I that organized. So the question arises of whether to blow out the candle or leave it to burn. Or should you use a snuffer to extinguish the flame, or perhaps your fingers (ouch)?

Well first, *never* leave the candle to burn down alone. This has nothing to do with magic—it is just common sense. Any flame should be thought of as a toddler—unpredictable and capable of destroying everything in your home in a flash!

There is a school of thought that says you should never blow out a candle used in magic; some think that this blows out the essence of the light created by the flame. I am not of this school at all! I believe the essence of magic is you yourself. And what could be more magical than your own breath? I always blow out my candles if I can't leave them to burn down. And I always take that moment as an opportunity to mix my breath with the spell that has just been cast and to send thanks for its successful working. I see this as a perfect moment to give a final personal touch to what I have been doing and to rightly send thanks for any help the spell may have received. Manners are everything here!

If you choose to use a snuffer or your fingers, that's good too. It's all a matter of personal preference. A bent spoon can make a wonderful snuffer, but please be careful with the fingers thing. Pain is not necessary in spell casting!

So now that you know the basics of candle magic, you have a wealth of possibilities available to you for using this way of spell casting. Take it slowly and find out what works for you. But if you want to experiment, here are a few ideas that I use:

- *Write words.* Write down your spell on a piece of paper and burn it in the candle flame (always remembering those fingers—get some tongs). You can get really fancy here, with different colored paper for each type of spell if you like, but I always use white. Try writing just a few simple words to start. You can progress to more elaborate verses as you get more experienced. Remember, words are an extremely powerful thing and you must think carefully before writing them down. Be sure of your intent and state it plainly.

- *Wind thread.* Wrap a piece of thread around your candle before lighting it. Imagine that your intent is spiraling with the thread. This can be a great focus and a wonderful way to create something to carry with you at the end of your spell to keep it going. Spells for confidence and money in particular can become more effective if you carry part of them with you. At the end of the burning, take the thread and some of the wax with you and carry it in a small pouch so you have it on hand whenever you need a boost.

- *Sprinkle herbs.* A pinch of an appropriate herb sprinkled into the flame during the spell can add the power of that herb to your work. There is a list of common herbs and their associations in the appendix. Keep some small jars or bags of dried herbs especially for this purpose. Dried herbs certainly work better in the flame and are quite often cheaper. And they are certainly a lot easier to store. Remember to use only a pinch, however. It's the magical element of these herbs you are using here. Any more and you're playing with fire, literally!

- *Give thanks.* Don't forget to light a candle of thanks. So often, we get caught up in what we are doing in spell work and forget all about that purest of intentions—to give thanks. I like to light a candle in the evening. I do it almost every day and I use this moment to send out thanks and healing to all that need it. Just focus that intent into the candle and light it in the same way as before. If we all did this a little more, I really believe it could make a huge difference in the world. Send out that warm healing vibe as often as you can to all you can. It is one of the most important parts of who we are and what we do with our magic!

Witchy Ways to Celebrate February

- Decorate your home and altar with candles to welcome the return of the sun. Place a pot of bulbs in your home as your magical focus.

- Make Brighid dolls from stems of straw; light a fire to welcome in the new.

- Get out and about to search for signs of spring (wrap up warm, though).

- This is a good time to find a wand, so hunt for the one that's meant for you and spend time focusing on it and making it individual to you.

- Organize your Book of Shadows to get ready for the start of the spring.

- Cook with milk to celebrate the ewe's milk of the season.

- Use candle magic to spell for the stirrings of spring and any tiny flickers of ideas that may grow.

February Folklore

"When the cat lies in the sun in February, she will creep behind the stove in March."

"Of all the months of the year, curse a fair February."

"If it thunders in February, it will frost in April."

"If February gives much snow, a fine summer it doth foreshow!"

FINAL THOUGHTS

Oh my goodness, we've made it through the entire year, my lovelies. Can you believe it? I really hope you had a nice time rambling through the months with me. And I hope I didn't lose you too often along the way!

With all that we've looked at around the Wheel of the Year, the one thing I really hope you all take away from this book is confidence. Believe in yourself. You are a wonderful, magical being full of potential and life. Dance when you can. Sing out with joy. Find magic in the world. And most important—eat chocolate. Go on, you know you want to!

Blessings,

Mandy

xxx

Magical Properties of Herbs, Plants, and Trees

Each tree and plant has its own magical properties. Knowing what these are can help you to work your magic more effectively. Here are the lists of properties that I work from most often. They are by no means exhaustive!

I don't think you can beat *Cunningham's Encyclopedia of Magical Herbs* if you want extensive information on what each herb, spice, or tree can do, but I like to keep things simple. Below are the properties that resonate with me when I charge magical ingredients and materials. If you are charging something and you feel that it holds different properties for you, then use it for the magical purpose that speaks to you. These lists are only intended as a good place to start.

Herbs and Plants

Angelica: protection

Basil: love and luck

Bay: strength

Borage: courage

Caraway: anti-theft

Cardamom: lust

Catnip: cat magic and happiness

Chamomile: sleep and calming

Chickweed: fertility

Chili: hex-breaking

Cinnamon: power

Cleavers: commitment

Cloves: positivity

Clover (red): luck

Comfrey: protection

Coriander: health

Cowslip: youth

Cumin: peace of mind

Daisy: love

Dandelion: wishes

Dill: protection

Dock: healing

Elderflowers and elderberries: blessings and protection

Eucalyptus: healing

Fennel: purification

Feverfew: good health

Garlic: protection

Ginger: power

Ground ivy: divination

Grass: psychic powers

Herb Robert: stability

Hops: sleep and health

Horseradish: purification

Juniper: exorcism

Lavender: peace

Lemongrass: lust

Lovage: love

Mace: mental power

Marigold: prophetic dreams

Marjoram: happiness

Meadowsweet: peace

Mint: money and cleansing

Mustard: protection

Nettle: courage

Olive: potency

Pansy: children's magic

Parsley: purification

Pepper: protection

Peppermint: psychic powers

Plantain: strength and health

Poppy: fertility

Primrose: love

Rose: red/passion, pink/true love

Rosemary: cleansing and memory

Saffron: gentleness

Sage: wisdom and protection

St. John's wort: mood-lifting

Savory: mental powers

Sloe: exorcism

Star anise: luck

Wild strawberry: sweet love

Tansy: longevity

Tea: wealth

Thistle: strength

Thyme: healing

Turmeric: purification

Valerian: sleep

Vanilla: mental powers and female magic

Violet: peace

Wormwood: spirits

Yarrow: courage and dispelling sorrow

TREES

Ash: prosperity

Aspen: anti-theft

Bamboo: luck

Beech: wishes

Birch: new beginnings

Blackberry: fairy magic

Buckthorn: official matters

Cypress: easing of grief

Elder: the Goddess

Elm: elf magic

Hawthorn: fertility and magic

Holly: dream magic

Horse chestnut: money

Larch: male magic

Lilac: exorcism

Oak: strength

Palm: potency

Pine: success

Raspberry: pregnancy magic

Rowan: protection

Walnut: mental powers

Willow: water magic and moon magic

Yew: death and rebirth.

Magical Property

Anti-theft: aspen, caraway

Blessing: elderflowers and elderberries

Calming: chamomile

Cat magic: catnip

Children's magic: pansy

Cleansing: mint, rosemary

Commitment: cleavers

Courage: borage, nettle, yarrow

Death: yew

Divination: ground ivy

Dream magic: holly

Elf magic: elm

Exorcism: juniper, lilac, sloe

Fairy magic: blackberry

Female magic: vanilla

Fertility: chickweed, hawthorn, poppy, raspberry

Gentleness: saffron

Goddess: elder

Grief: cypress

Happiness: marigold

Healing: dock, eucalyptus, thyme

Health: coriander, feverfew, hops, plantain

Hex-breaking: chili

Longevity: tansy

Love, true: pink rose

Love: basil, daisy, lovage, primrose, wild strawberry

Luck: bamboo, basil, clover (red), star anise

Lust: cardamom, lemongrass

Magic: hawthorn

Memory: rosemary

Mental power: mace, savory, vanilla, walnut

Money: horse chestnut, mint

Mood-lifting: St. John's wort

Moon magic: willow

New beginnings: birch

Official matters: buckthorn

Passion: red rose

Peace: lavender, meadowsweet, violet

Peace of mind: cumin

Positivity: cloves

Potency: olive, palm

Power: cinnamon, ginger

Prophetic dreams: marigold

Prosperity: ash

Protection: angelica, comfrey, dill, elderflowers and elderberries, garlic, mustard, pepper, rowan, sage

Psychic power: grass, peppermint

Purification: fennel, horseradish, parsley, turmeric

Rebirth: yew

Sleep: chamomile, hops, valerian

Sorrow: yarrow

Spirits: wormwood

Stability: Herb Robert

Strength: bay, oak, plantain, thistle

Success: pine

Water magic: willow

Wealth: tea

Wisdom: sage

Wishes: beech, dandelion

Youth: cowslip

ACKNOWLEDGMENTS

This book would never have been written if it hadn't been for some very special people who really deserve huge thank-yous and big squidgy hugs. First, I need to thank two special friends, Robert Kyle and Steve Smith, who created the Hedgewitch Cooks website and continue to work on the project to this day. Robert, I especially thank you for the wonderful couplets that grace the start of each chapter. Thank you both so much for all the help and support you have given me. And a big thank-you goes to Amber and the team at RedWheel/Weiser for having faith in this book from the very start, and for being so lovely. To my friends Karen (the mad one) and my original Hedgewitch, Judith, thank you for inspiring me!

I also need to thank my wonderful patient family—my girls, Alexandra and Bethany; my beautiful grandbabies, Fae, Ella, and Ruby; my brother, Michael; and most of all, my long-suffering husband, Mr. Hedgewitch himself, Stewart. He has encouraged me, supported me, and brought me endless coffees to keep me going! Stewart, I love you, bun.

Another big thank-you goes to my lovely online family, however and wherever our paths have crossed. I am so blessed to have had so much support from you all.

Last, but not least, to everyone who has taken the trouble to read this book—thank you all. I hope you found something useful within it. You guys are all amazing!

ABOUT THE AUTHOR

Mandy Mitchell is a mother, a doting grandma, and also a practicing Hedgewitch. She lives within the magical landscape of Wiltshire, with Stonehenge, Avebury, and Savernake forest very close by. She believes in juggling real life and trying to live each day magically by turning the day-to-day tasks into magical rituals. Along with simple spells, seasonal food, and honoring the rhythms of nature, a sense of humor is key to being a modern Hedgewitch!

Mandy is passionate about connecting with others in today's busy world, bringing the modern and ancient together. She embraces the online world and would love to hear from anyone wishing to be part of the magical community. Check her out: *facebook.com/hedgewitchbookofdays*

TO OUR READERS